THIS BOOK BELONGS TO:

DEAN + BENNY

KEEP THE MAGIC ALIVE! - Will Fern.

Our Magic Mission:

Empower children by teaching them the art of magic; building character, confidence & communication skills for life.

Illustrations By: Enroc illustration Studio

Special thanks to Rebekah South, Caitlyn Rosander, JT South, Dal Sanders, Daniel Fox, Sydney Mac, Michelle Walker, Laura Bangerter, and all the dedicated Discover Magic Presenters around the world.

Published by Discover Magic and Printed in China
www.**DiscoverMagic**.com

Dear Future Magician,

Welcome to the wonderful world of MAGIC. I have filled this book with some of the most extraordinary activities that I could devise. As you explore these pages you will begin to experience what MAGIC is all about . . . FUN!

You see, MAGIC shares many of the same qualities as games and puzzles. Think about it. One of the reasons we love puzzles is because they pique our curiosity. And MAGIC, like a game, captivates our attention creating the excitement of not knowing what will happen next.

To help you get started on your journey, I have placed several top-secret file folders from my magic vault inside this book. These file folders will reveal to you some of magic's most guarded secrets as well as tell you about some legendary magicians.

One last thing... the mysteries and fun contained in this book are meant to be shared, so grab a pencil, grab a friend and get ready for an amazing adventure.

Magically your friend,

Mr. Magic

P.S. To learn even more magic, get trained by a professional and become an incredible true magician, visit: **DiscoverMagic.com**

you are the magic

Look throughout this letter and find the letters that have been underlined to discover Mr. Magic's secret message.

FUN
GUIDE

Mr. Magic's Favorite...

Puzzles

Easy

Medium

Hard

Magic Tricks

Beginner

Intermediate

Advanced

Optical illusions

THE MAGIC SHOP

Not everything is what it seems to be in the magic shop. Can you find all the hidden items?

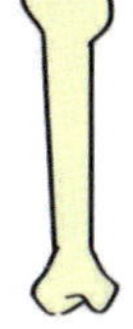

Dog Bone

Ant Farm

Seashell

Can of Tuna

Gallon of Milk

Key

Doughnut

Shoe

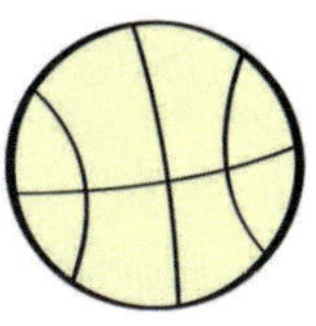

Basket Ball

Tennis Racket

Slice of Pizza

Taco

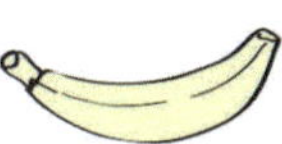

Banana

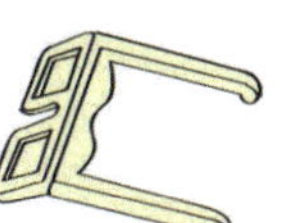

Sun Glasses

Fish

CHAIN ESCAPE
START
Mr. Magic has found himself trapped in chains. See if you can help him escape. Start in the center and work your way out.

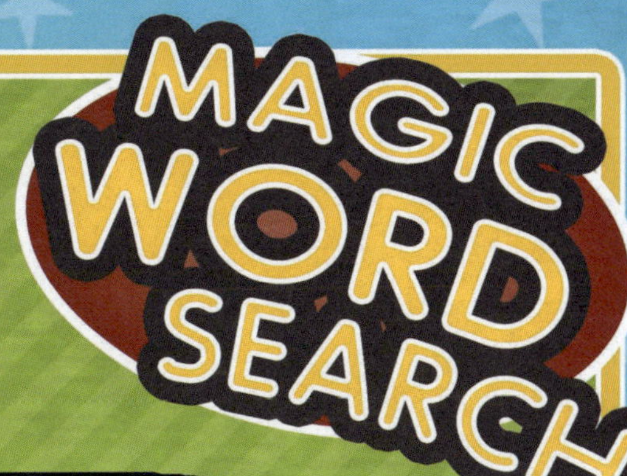

Eight pretend magic words and eight words that really work magic are hidden in this bubble.

Look up, down, and diagonal to see if you can find them all!

U I A B Z Z T W L L L I K E S P R C C H

O F F Y Y D Y R J P T N E B F H N J Z O

B O M E D L S G V O L R Y B E W D B G C

V R O J R H D T M Z Q S A M K D V J H U

M G U C N M F R I P C H A L N Q Y H N S

Y I M Z R Q A N V N L S M P A Y K S J P

G V F I V S N H U J E E K R U K L L W O

M E D T N F J O Q S J M A E R S A D O C

P Y I V B O Y N N U O W Y S K H R Z M U

G O J G L K A E J X Z G Z T E A M B A S

G U I L N E P F J R C K I O U Z B V N M

E G E A O O J D D O W T S C M A G I C S

S H H X V A I M S O R R Y H A M A A K K

F T H A B R A C A D A B R A K N Z F B D

O Q B U I U N D E R S T A N D D E J K L

G R E A T J O B U C P X N G G X A I A O

Q Q L X W I C Z E L D Z N O T V F G E V

E K K X O H T F S I M S A L A B I M O P

Pretend Magic Words

Abracadabra
Shazam
Sim Sala Bim
Presto Chango
Open Sesame
Sarmoti
Alakazam
Hocus Pocus

Real Magic Words

Hello
Please
Thank You
I'm Sorry
I Forgive You
I Understand
Great Job
I Can

Mr. Magic is really good at reading people's minds.

Can you tell what they are thinking too?

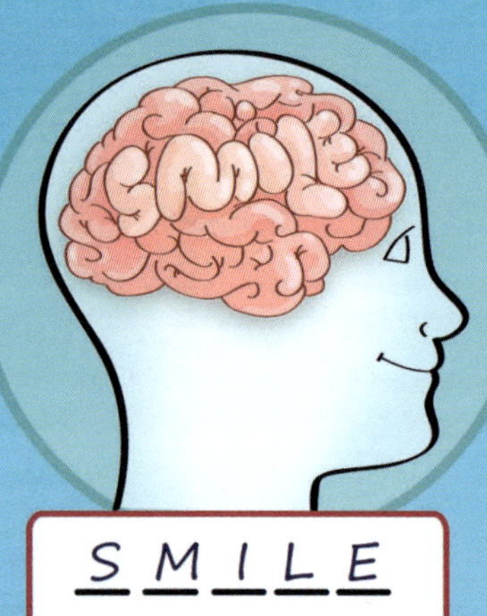

S M I L E

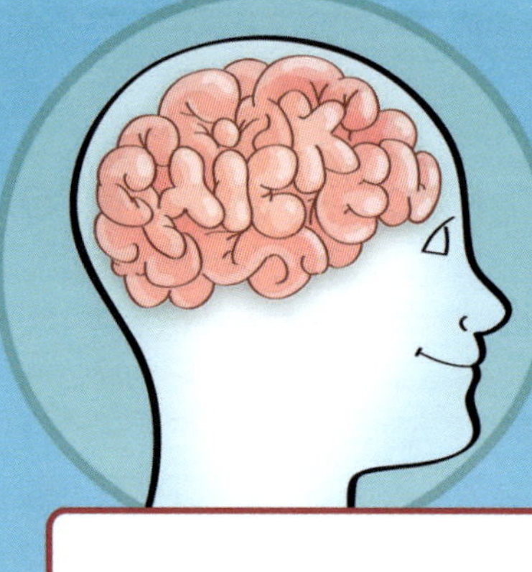

_ _ _ _ _ _ _

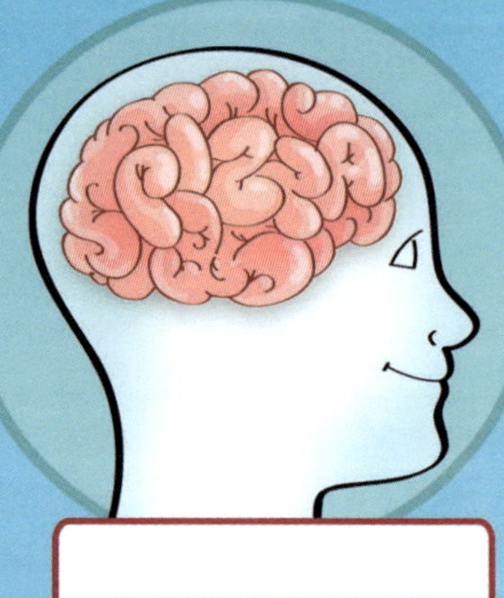

_ _ _ _ _

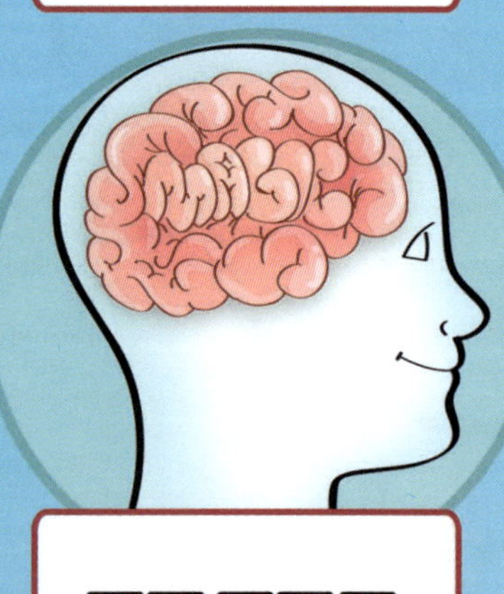

_ _ _ _ _

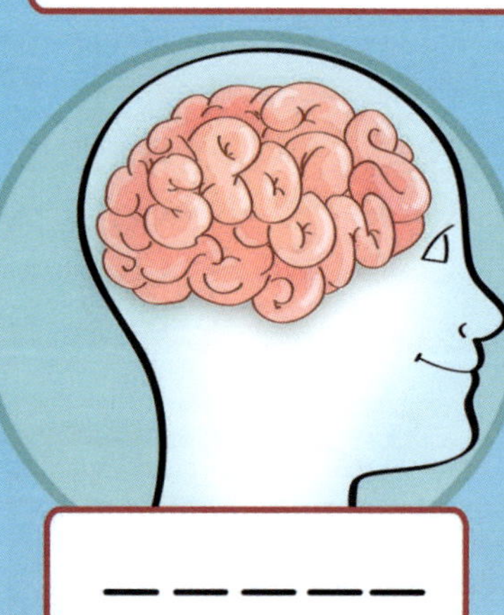

_ _ _ _ _

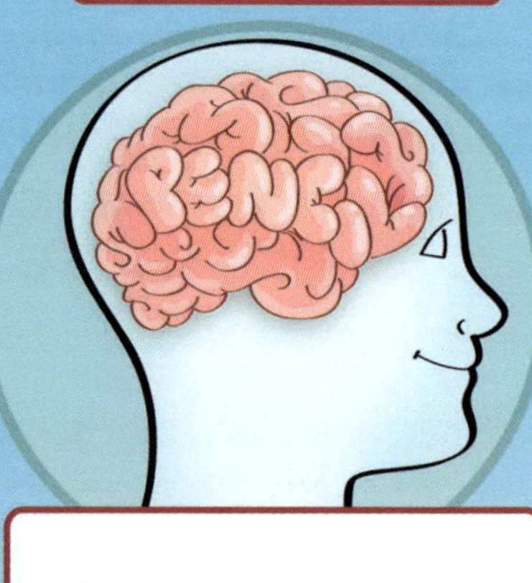

_ _ _ _ _ _

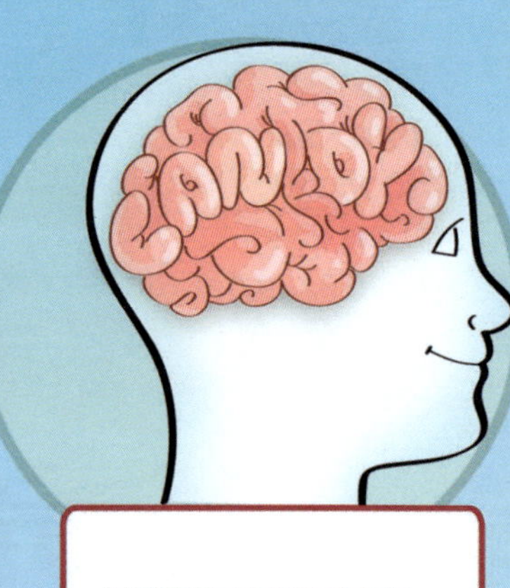

_ _ _ _ _

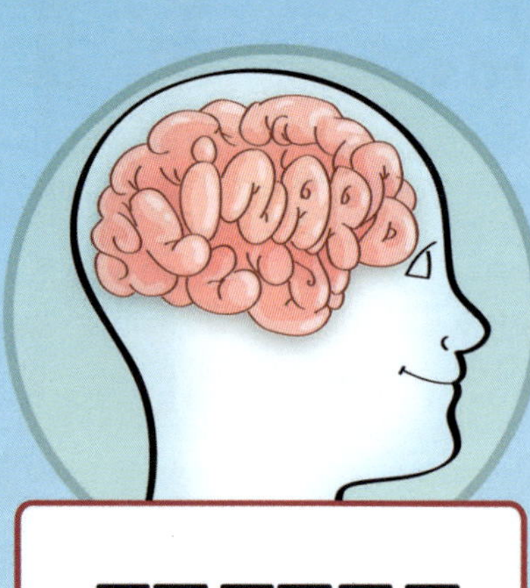

_ _ _ _ _ _

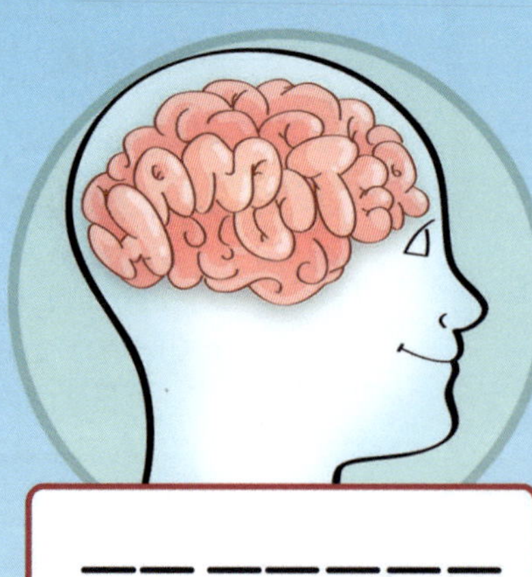

_ _ _ _ _ _ _

PICK A CARD

Now let's see if Mr. Magic can read your mind. Follow the instructions below and then turn the page to see if he's right!

1. Pick any red card.
2. Move left or right to the nearest black card.
3. Move up or down to the nearest red card.
4. Move diagonally to the nearest black card.
5. Move left or right to the nearest red card.
6. Remember this card.

Can you draw four straight lines and connect all nine dots?

Mr. Magic left you a secret message. Tilt the top of this book toward the ground and close one eye to see if you can read it.

IS THIS YOUR CARD?

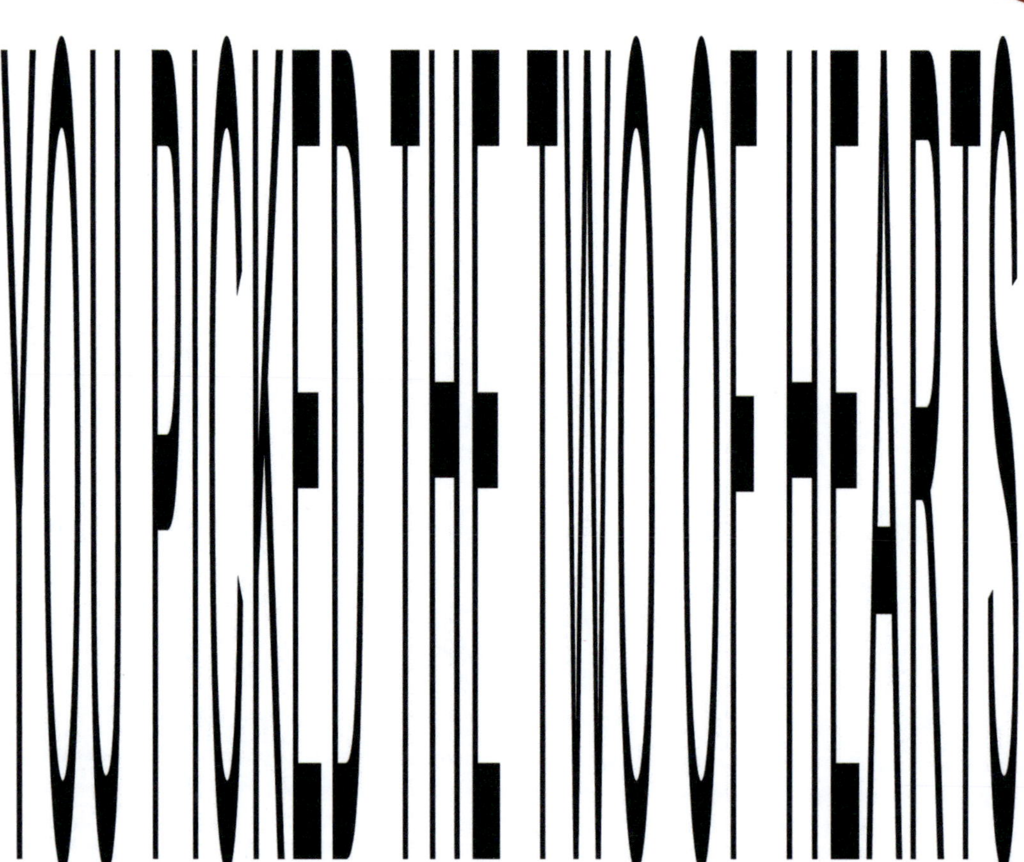

Stare at these boxes... Do you see flashing dots?

Make an Optical Illusion

Connect the dots below and see what popular illusion you create.

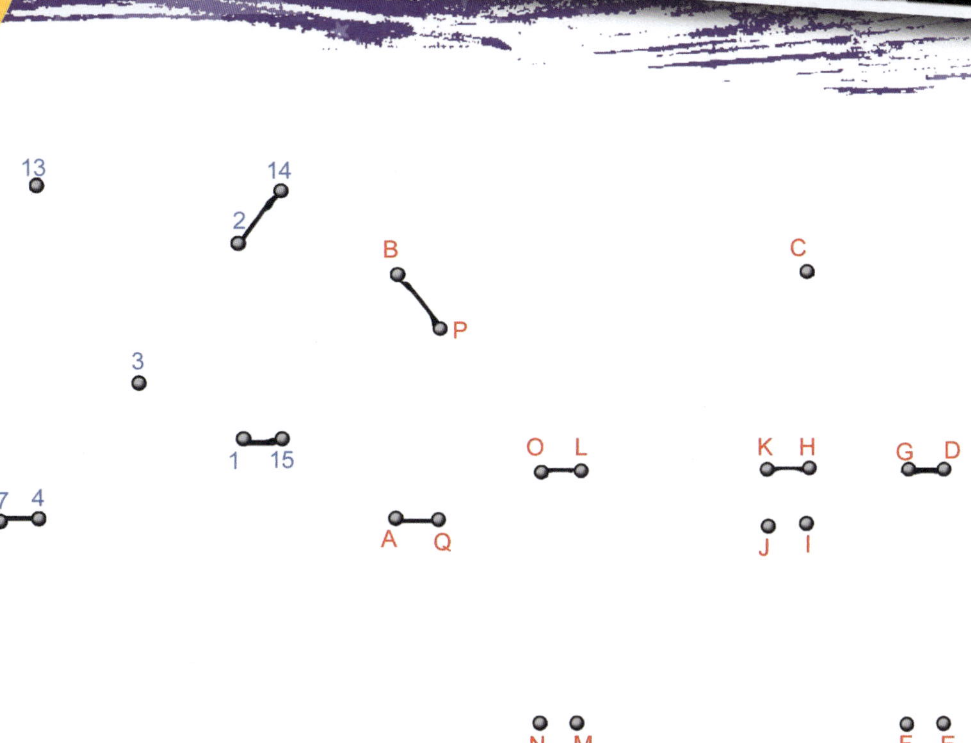

Which table do you think is bigger?

A: Believe it or not they are the same size.

*Try it out. Trace a table top on a piece of paper and put it over the other.

A true magician
Joanie Spina

Born: August 4, 1953
Boston, Massachusetts, USA

Background:

Joanie Spina was respectful. She always treated others how she wanted to be treated. Not only was she an amazing magician, but she was also a remarkable director—always knowing what to say and do to make others shine.

Famous Fact:

Joanie Spina worked for star magician, David Copperfield, for over ten years and helped direct some of his most incredible illusions including flying and walking through the Great Wall of China.

Quote:

"It's not about the magic trick, it's about the person performing and what they do with it that makes it magical."

Joanie Spina
True Trait: Respectful

Did you know?

The paperclip was invented by several people in different countries around the same period of time.

The world's largest paperclip was displayed in Oslo, Norway in 1989, and is about 23 feet tall.

MAKING THE CHANGE

Find out how on page 79

Betcha...

Get six coins and place them on the table as shown here. A row of four coins crossed by a row of three coins.

Bet you can't rearange these six coins so that you have two rows of four coins each.

LEARN MAGIC

S3CRET5

Linking Paperclips

The Effect:

Two paperclips are placed separately on a slip of paper. Then, when you pull on the ends, the clips fly off of the paper and are linked together.

The Secret:

The secret is in the placement of the paperclips on the folded slip of paper.

Materials Needed:

Two large paperclips and a slip of paper or dollar bill

Presentation:

"Here I have the Cannonball Brothers." (show paperclips) "When they are shot into the air from opposite sides of the stage, they can magically catch each other in midair... It's AMAZING and it only costs a dollar. Wanna see?"

Fold the bill one third of the way over and place the first paperclip as shown here.

Now fold the other third of the bill back over making an "s" shape and place another paperclip on the bill clipping the middle part of the bill to the part you just folded over as shown here.

Now on the count of three, pull on the two ends of the bill "BOOM," sending them flying into the air and linking together.

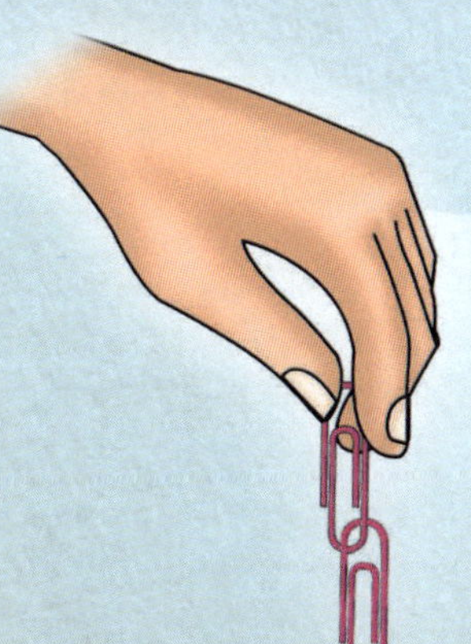

PICTURE RIDDLES

1 What has 88 keys, but can't open a door?

2 What gets wetter the more it dries?

3 What has an eye but cannot see?

4 What never asks a question, but always gets answered?

5 What can go for miles yet doesn't even move?

6 What can go around the world, yet always stays in one corner?

7 What has four legs, but only one foot?

8 What starts with E and ends with E and has one letter in it?

9 What room has no walls, no doors, no floors, and no windows?

10 What has a face and two hands but no arms or legs?

11 What gets whiter the dirtier it gets?

12 What has to be broken before you can use it?

ANSWERS

___ 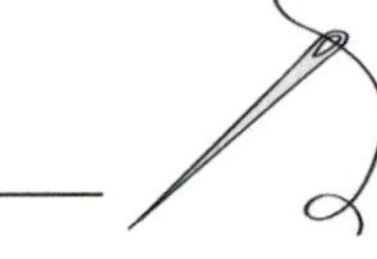 ___   ___  ___ 

___ 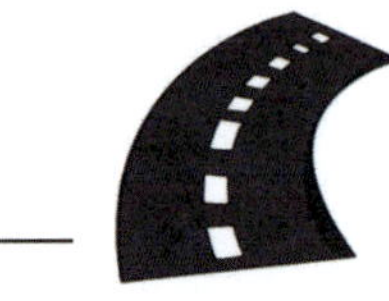 ___ 

___  ___ 

___  ___  ___  ___ 

Can you unscramble these letters to make an animal appear?
Make sure you "spell" them correctly.

FEGIRFA	Giraffe	USOME	
NOCORAC		LAHEW	
POPMATHIPSUO		LETRUT	
ANTLEPHE		HINPLOD	
BEZRA		KEYNOD	
GRETI		LIDROCOCE	
NOMYEK		GONLAMIF	
TAGLOIRAL		HEPES	
KANES		RUTYEK	
BITBAR		NUGPINE	
SHEMTAR		UKNKS	

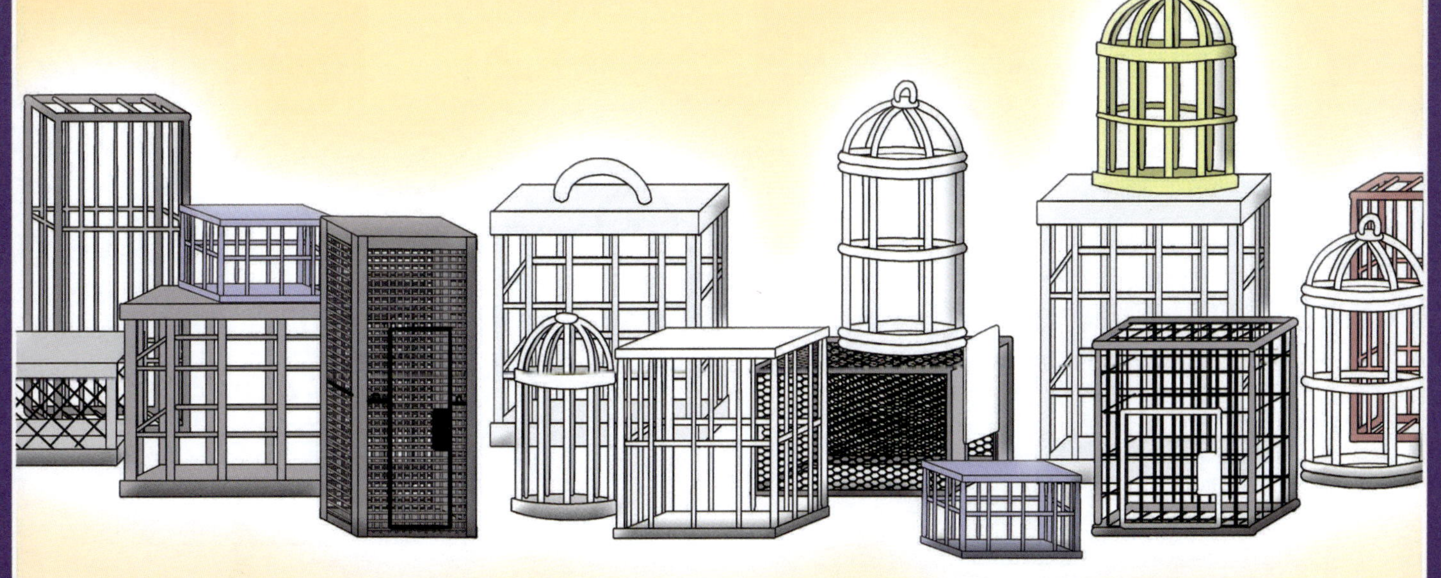

BIRD JOKES

Q: What do you call a magic owl?
A: Hooodini!

Q: What do you call a very rude bird?
A: A mockingbird!

Q: What do you call a sick eagle?
A: Illegal!

Q: What birds do you usually find locked up?
A: Jail-birds!

Q: What do you call a bunch of chickens playing hide-&-seek?
A: Fowl play!

Q: What kind of bird doesn't need a comb?
A: A bald eagle!

Q: What kind of bird can carry the most weight?
A: A crane!

Q: What do you get if you cross a duck with a firework?
A: Firequacker!

Put the bird back in the cage. Stare at the dot and slowly move the page towards your nose.

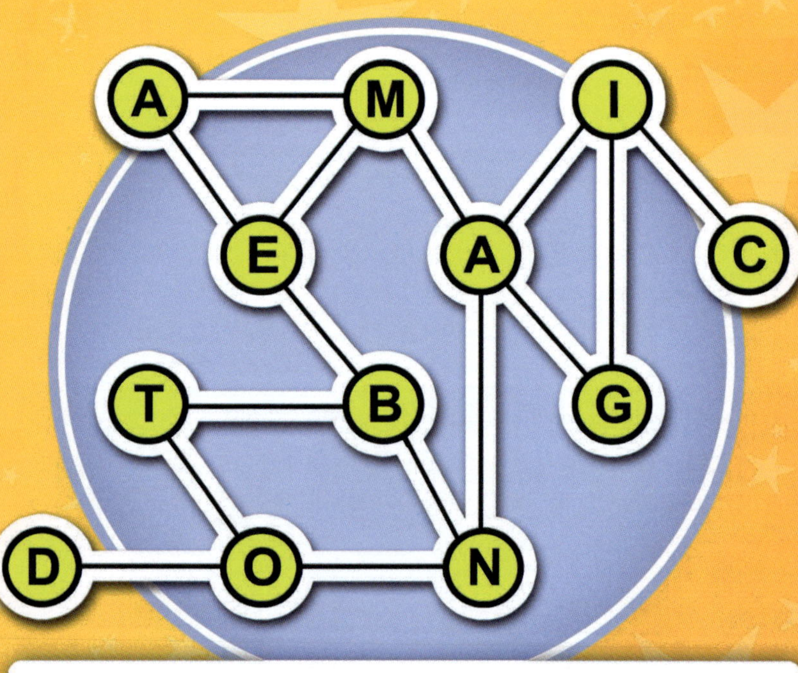

SAWING A LADY IN HALF

Can you match up the two halves of these eight famous ladies?

Cleo	eAusten
Moth	ank
AnneFr	patra
Jan	aParks
Susan	eller
HelenK	B.Anthony
Amel	iaEarhart
Ros	erTeresa

The horizontal lines look a little tilted, but in reality they are parallel.

Can you figure out the word or phrase each of these represents?

FOODS

THE MAGIC SHOW

Not everything is what it seems to be in the magic show. Can you find all the hidden items?

MR MAGIC'S
SHOW OF WONDER

MR MAGIC
SHOW OF WONDER

Microphone

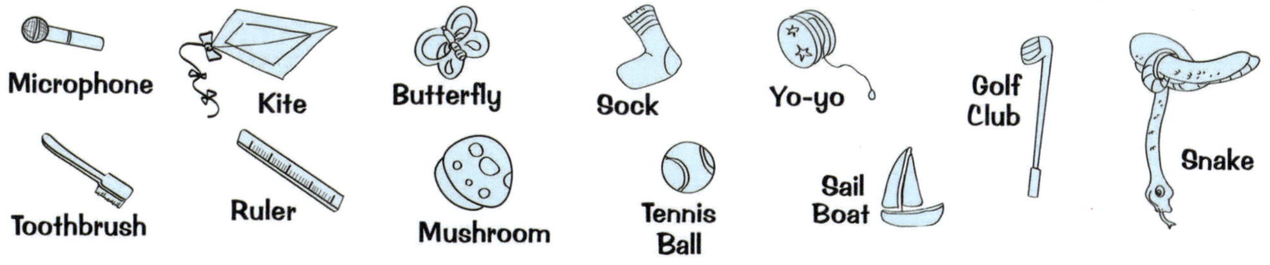

Kite

Butterfly

Sock

Yo-yo

Golf Club

Snake

Toothbrush

Ruler

Mushroom

Tennis Ball

Sail Boat

A true magician
Max Malini

Born: August 14, 1873
Ostrow, Poland, Europe

Background:

Max Malini was prepared. He was best known for impromptu magic. Although it seemed improvised, the truth is, he went to great lengths by always planning ahead and having everything setup beforehand.

Famous Fact:

Malini's hands were so small they couldn't even cover a playing card. He was well known for being able to make a block of ice appear from anybody's hat at any time.

Quote:

"I wait until the time is right. If necessary I wait a week!"

Max Malini
True Trait: Prepared

Photo courtesy Nielsen Magic Collection

Did you know?

One of Saturn's moons has ice volcanoes!

It happens when ice deep below the surface gets heated and turned into a vapor that then erupts into the moon's chilly atmosphere as ice cubes.

DON'T TIP THE BOTTLE

Find out how on page 79

Betcha...

Place a bottle upside down in the very center of a piece of paper.

Bet you can't get the paper out from under the bottle without touching the bottle or knocking it over.

S3CRET5

Instant Ice

The Effect:
Turn water into ice in seconds.

The Secret:
A cup is prepared with a hidden sponge and a few ice cubes.

Materials:
2 cups (Not see-through)
sponges, scissors, ice and water

Preparation:

1. Cut the sponge to fit in the bottom of a cup nicely. Make sure you have enough sponge to absorb all the water you will pour in the cup.
2. Place three ice cubes in the cup with the sponge.
3. Put just a little water in the second cup.

Presentation:
"I once travelled to Alaska and went into an abandoned ice cave, and found one of the biggest icicles ever. I wanted to see how cold it was, so I took off my gloves and touched it with one finger. Lucky for me I didn't get frostbite, but I can show you what I did get." (Pour the small amount of water from the cup into the cup with the secret ice cubes.) "The ability to turn water into... (Place hand that touched icicle over cup and then pick it up and pour the ice out.) ...ICE."

LINKING WORDS

Fill in the blanks with the linking word that can be used to create two separate phrases. Example: Tree Top Hat making Tree Top & Top Hat Use the answers to fill in the crossword puzzle.

DOWN

1. Peanut ______________ Knife
2. Trash ______________ Opener
3. Magic ______________ Worm
4. Pepperoni ______________ Party
5. Tree ___Top___ Hat
6. Horse ______________ Lace
7. Pig ______________ Pal
8. Revolving ______________ Bell
9. Arm ______________ Stop
10. Cotton ______________ Apple
11. Bottled ______________ Melon
12. Cannon ______________ Game

ACROSS

1. Hot Air ______________ Animal
2. Copy ______________ Fish
3. Shark ______________ Paste
4. Toilet ______________ Airplane
5. Mouse ______________ Door
6. Vanilla ______________ Truck
7. Piano ______________ Chain
8. Corn ______________ House
9. Rail ______________ Runner

Miss-Tree Forest!

Look at this picture for 30 seconds. Memorize as much as you can, then turn the page and see how much you can remember.

HOCUS FOCUS

Miss-Tree Forest Quiz!

(From previous page)

1. What is eating the pizza?
2. What is floating in the water?
3. What color is the carrot tree?
4. How many doughnut trees are there?
5. How many sprinkles are on each donut?
6. What color are the clouds?
7. What color is the bird?
8. How many slices of pizza are there?

WISHING WELL

Make a wish and pick a coin. Follow that coin's trail. If it makes it into the well, your wish might come true!

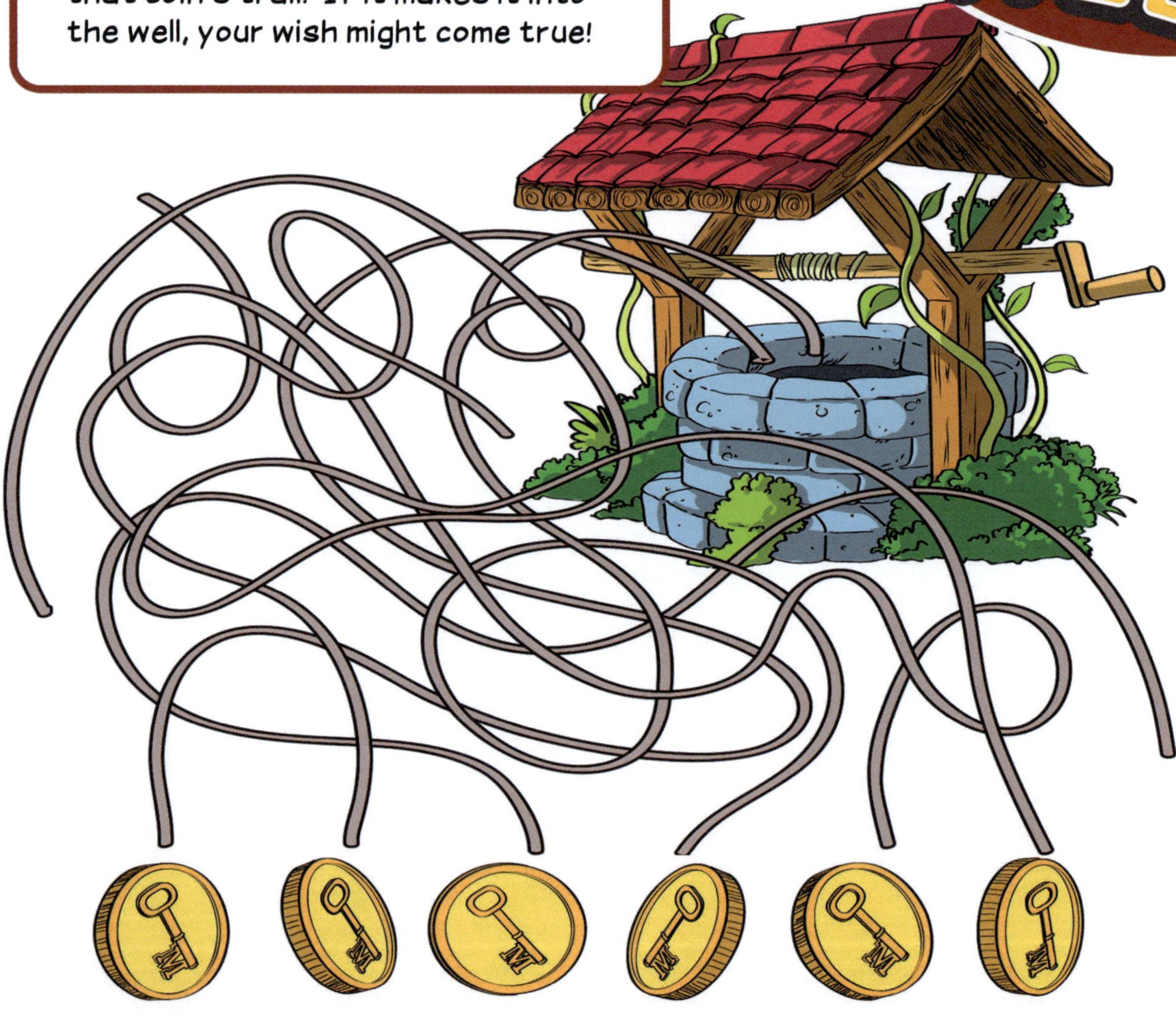

Which spot is in the very center?

One of the Acrobatic Jacks lost his balance. Can you help him find his center?

Three of these puzzle cubes are the same. Can you figure out which cube is not the same as the others?

BEFORE BACK STAGE

AFTER

Mr. Magic decided to clean up backstage. Can you find the 12 differences from before and after he cleaned up?

BAG OF TRICKS

Can you find four items that appear in all three bags?

What am I? I have keys but no locks. I have space but no room. You can enter on one side but must escape in the corner.

Write down EVERY OTHER letter as you go around the safe to crack the code.

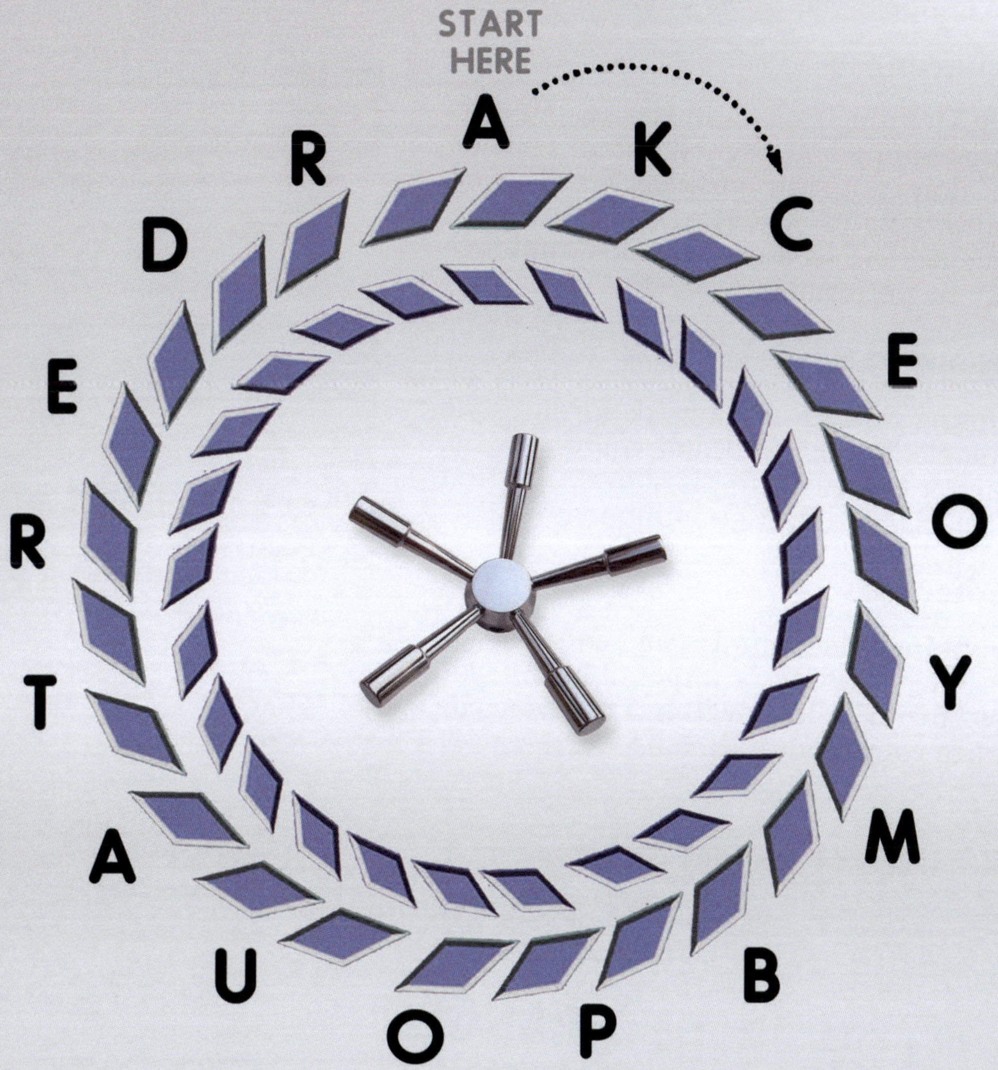

START HERE

A K C E O Y M B P O U A T R E D R

ANSWER: A ________ ________.

Stare at the center of the safe. Move your head forward and back. Do you see the circles turning?

A true magician
Doug Henning

Born: May 3, 1947
Winnipeg, Manitoba, Canada

Background:

Doug Henning was enthusiastic. He was always happy and excited about what he was doing. Using positive words and smiling with his eyes were his trademarks. Doug seemed as amazed as his audience when he performed his magic.

Famous Fact:

Henning won several awards for his style of magic by adding bright colors, music, dance & comedy into his shows. His first TV special had over 50 million viewers.

Quote:

"Anything the mind can conceive is possible. Nothing is impossible. All you have to do is look within, and you can realize your fondest dreams."

Doug Henning
True Trait: Enthusiastic

Did you know?

Rubber bands were patented in 1845.

Rubber bands release heat energy when stretched, but absorb heat energy when retracted.

YELLOW BLUE ORANGE
BLACK RED GREEN
PURPLE YELLOW RED
ORANGE GREEN BLACK
BLUE RED PURPLE
GREEN BLUE ORANGE

Betcha...

Bet you can't go through this list and only say the COLOR not the WORD!

It is really hard. Your right brain tries to say the color but your left brain insists on reading the word!

Jumping Bands

The Effect:

Rubber bands jump magically from around your fingers to the other side of your hand.

The Secret:

There is a secret move. The rubber band that jumps is stretched out and the tips of all four fingers of that hand are placed in that rubber band as you close your hand into a fist.

When you open your hand the rubber band will automatically jump to the other fingers.

SECRET VIEW

Materials:

2 rubber bands (Different colors)

Presentation:

"Here I have some different colored rubber bands from the wild west. Don't worry they're not bandits. Please pick one of them you would like to see jump on the band wagon." (Show your fist and move it as if it is a wagon. They pick one.) "Great! This is the one you want to see jump? I will pick another to help tell yours when to jump." (Place both bands on fingers and do the secret move.) "On the count of three we are going to say 'yee hah.' Ready? Watch as this band will jump from the back to the front of this band wagon. 1,2,3 'yee hah'!" (Open your hand revealing it has jumped.)

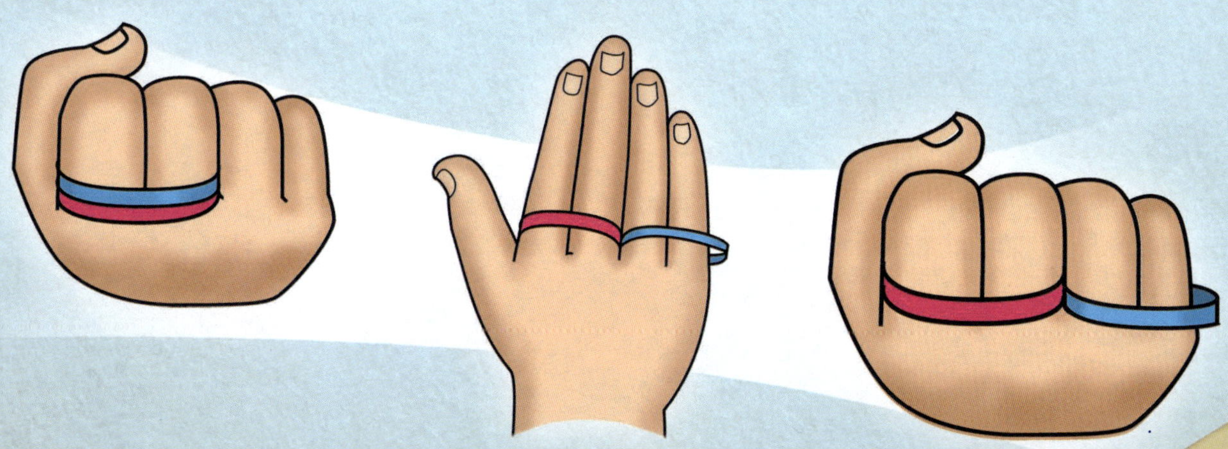

Elephant Jokes

Q: What do you get when you cross a potato with an elephant?
A: Mashed potatoes!

Q: Why don't elephants like playing cards in the jungle?
A: Because of all the cheetahs!

Q. Why don't elephants use computers?
A. They're afraid of the mouse!

Q: What happens when elephants get lightheaded?
A: They ele-faint!

Q: How do elephants talk to each other long distance?
A: On the elephone!

Q: What's an elephant's favorite vegetable?
A: Squash!

Q: What does a doctor give an elephant who's going to be sick?
A: Plenty of room!

Q: What is as big as an elephant, but weighs nothing?
A: The shadow of an elephant!

It might look like the scale is leaning on the elephant side, but it's not.

Can you tell which two jacks match exactly?

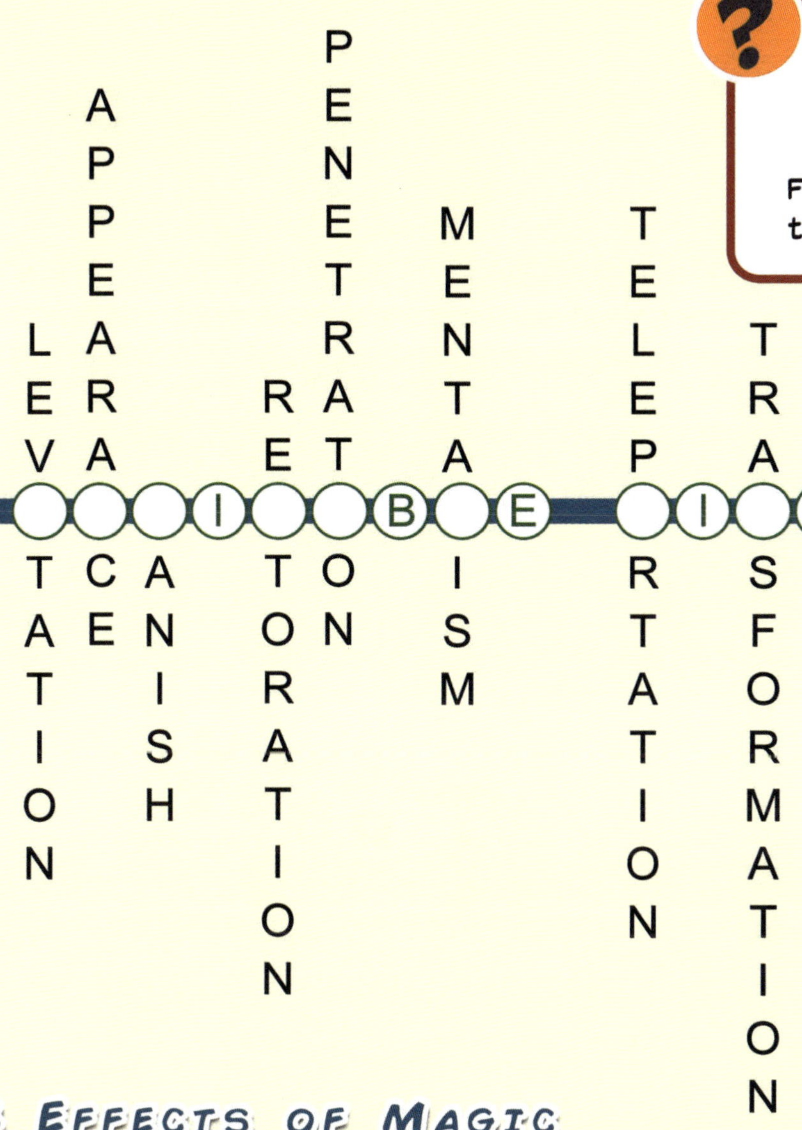

What do pigs use to write secret messages?

Fill in the blanks and complete the 8 effects of magic to find out.

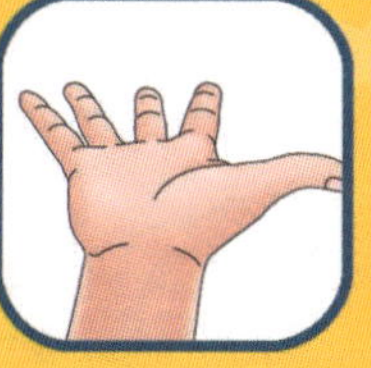

FANTASTIC BETCHAS

ARM SUPER STRONG

"Bet you can't lift my hand off the top of my head. Put your palm on the top of your head and instruct the person to try to remove it by pushing up on your forearm."

Secret: They won't be able to. It's physically impossible.

IMPOSSIBLE COIN FLIP

"Bet you I can flip a coin that is under a cup without touching the cup."

Secret: Place a coin heads up under a cup on a table. Wave your hands over the cup and hit the table as if you did it. When you friend picks up the cup to see. Turn the coin over- proving you could do it without you touching the cup.

NEVER SEEN BEFORE

"Bet I can show you something nobody has seen before. You are going to see it and then nobody will ever see it again."

Secret: A peanut. Crack it open and say, "No one has ever seen this one, (eat it) and no one will ever see it again."

DON'T SPILL A DROP

"Bet you I can drop eight coins into this full glass without any water spilling over."

Secret: Make sure the glass is filled to the brim with water. You'll be surprised to find that you can drop as many as 15-20 coins into a full glass before it spills over.

Stairway to NOWHERE

Which color step is the highest?

LOST IN THE DECK

Help Mr. Magic get through this maze of cards so that he can perform at the magic card castle.

MIX MATCH RIDDLES

1 What can you put in a bucket to make it lighter?

2 What building has the most stories?

3 What belongs to you but is used more by others?

4 What word becomes shorter if you add two letters to it?

5 What nail should you never hit with a hammer?

6 Everyone has it and no one can lose it, what is it?

7 What has no wings but flies?

8 What has never been seen, felt, or heard, yet has a name?

9 What can a person wear that is never out of style?

10 What gets harder to catch the faster you run?

11 What will you break if you name it?

12 What must you keep after giving it to someone else?

ANSWERS

____ A shadow
____ Your breath
____ Silence
____ Nothing
____ Holes
____ The library
____ A smile
____ Your word
____ Your fingernail
____ Your name
____ Short
____ Time

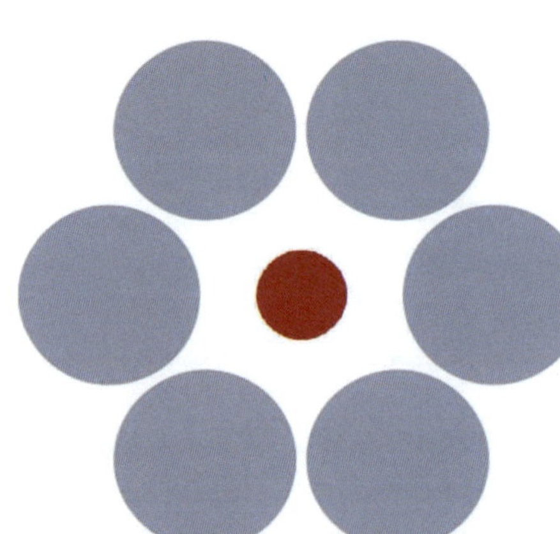

Which red dot looks bigger to you?

Don't believe your eyes. They are the same size!

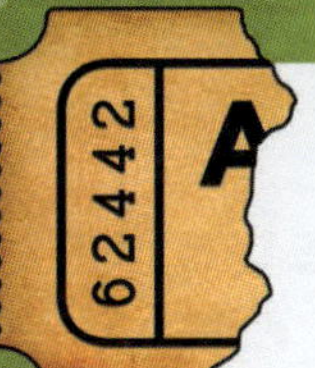

TERRIFIC TICKET

Can you match each of these ticket stubs to the correct other half?

CUPS & BALLS

Can you help Mr. Magic find all the words that have either "cup" or "ball" in them in this word search?

BUTTERCUP	BALLOON
HICCUP	BALLROOM
TEACUP	BALLERINA
CUPBOARD	MEATBALL
CUPCAKE	EYEBALL
OCCUPATION	SNOWBALL
OCCUPIED	VERBALLY
CUPID	GUMBALL

W X F B P H I C C U P N Z
S K B A L L E R I N A O S
N O F C G U M B A L L C S
O C G R T E A C U P T C Y
W C U P I D S F L R R U X
B U T T E R C U P R B P B
A P C U P B O A R D Z A A
L I C U P C A K E C L T L
L E M E A T B A L L M I L
L D B B A L L R O O M O O
O L J R E Y E B A L L N O
G D V E R B A L L Y W V N

FUTURE NUMBER

Follow the instructions to get a random number from the future not even YOU knew you would pick.

See if you can find the magic number in the crystal ball ten times.

Think of a three-digit number.
(The three numbers used must be different. i.e. 123)

Write it here:

___ ___ ___

Reverse that number:
(123 becomes 321)

___ ___ ___

Substract the smaller three-digit number from the larger:

Larger: ___ ___ ___
Smaller: – ___ ___ ___
Total: ___ ___ ___

Take the total and reverse that number.
(198 becomes 891)

Add the total to the reverse of the total and that is YOUR magic number!

Total: ___ ___ ___
Reverse: + ___ ___ ___
MAGIC #: ___ ___ ___

Can you figure out the word or phrase each of these represents?

ANYTHING
ANYTHING
ANYTHING
ANYTHING

A true magician
Harry Houdini

Born: March 24, 1874
Budapest, Hungary, Europe

Background:

Harry Houdini was confident. He believed in himself and knew he could do anything he put his mind to. Houdini made the art of escaping popular and was known as the greatest escape artist in the world.

Famous Fact:

Houdini was magic's greatest visionary. Harry created the longest-surviving organization of magicians in the world and was the longest running president of the Society of American Magicians.

Quote:

"What the eyes see and the ears hear, the mind believes."

Harry Houdini
True Trait: Confident

Did you know?

Ketchup can be used to polish things like coins, pots or pans.

Ketchup is acidic because of its tomatoes and vinegar. Some people rub it on brass items such as jewelry and lamps to remove tarnish. You can try it on an old penny!!!

TOOTHPICK BOXES

Find out how on page 79

Betcha...

Grab 16 toothpicks and set them up as shown here making five boxes.

Bet you can't move three toothpicks and make only four boxes.

S3CRET5

Floating Ketchup

The Effect:
You magically control a ketchup packet without touching it—making it rise or fall whenever you wish!

The Secret:
Secretly squeeze the bottle and the packet will sink. This works because a ketchup packet has an air bubble in it and when you squeeze the bottle you compress that air bubble—changing the density of the packet and causing it to sink.

Materials:
Ketchup packets, plastic bottle with cap, water

Preparation:

1. Collect several ketchup packets and test them by putting them into a bowl of water to find one that barely floats.
2. Place the ketchup packet into the bottle, fill the bottle 100% full of water, and screw the lid on tightly.
3. Squeeze the bottle gently to make sure you can make the ketchup packet dive deeper without too much effort.

Presentation:
Display the bottle with the ketchup packet sealed inside. Point out that the ketchup is floating at the top but you can cause it to move with your mind.

Gently squeeze the sides of the bottle, changing the pressure inside. The ketchup packet will slowly dive to the bottom of the bottle! Let go to make the ketchup rise again.

SHADOW PUPPETS

Can you guess what each animal is? Grab a flashlight and try one now!

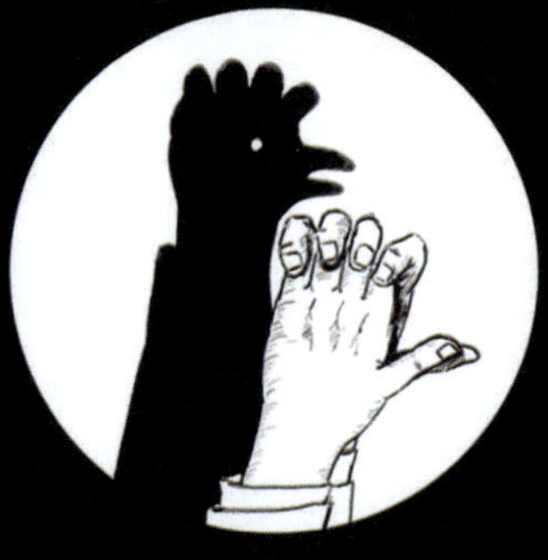

Which shadow matches the puppet exactly?

MAGIC SQUARES

Can you tell which one is a perfect square?

4	9	
3		7
		6

		2	13
	10		8
9	6	7	
4			

Fill in the box above with the numbers 1 - 9 so that each row across and up and down always adds up to 15.

Fill in the box to the side with the numbers 1 - 16 so that each row across and up and down always adds up to 34.

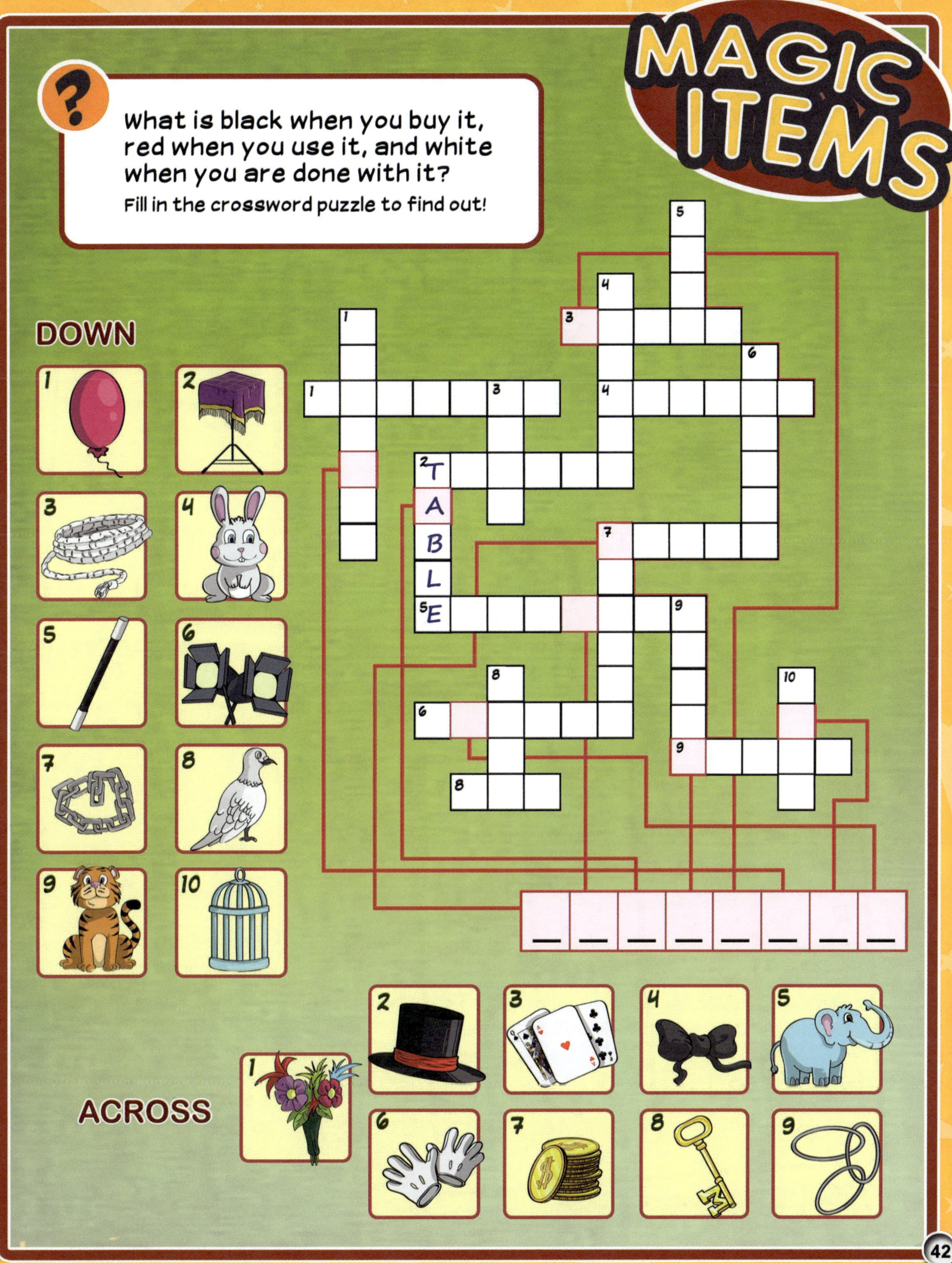
MAGIC ITEMS
What is black when you buy it, red when you use it, and white when you are done with it?
Fill in the crossword puzzle to find out!
DOWN
1 2 3 4 5 6 7 8 9 10
ACROSS
1 2 3 4 5 6 7 8 9
TABLE

EASY

G	I	F	T
		T	
	F	I	G

HARD

T	H	A	N	K	Y	O	U
N	O		U				
Y			T	U			
	U	Y	K				
		N	Y				O
					N		H
O					T	A	
				A	K	U	

HARD

B	I	R	T	H	D	A	Y
		A	Y		B	R	T
	A				R	H	I
R	T				A		
		Y				I	B
T	R	I				D	
H	Y	B		A	I		
	B			D	H	Y	

DIZZY DICE DASH

See who can get to the center first!

Each player picks a number 1-6, finds that number on the outside of the dice grid and races to the finish. Players can go up, down and diagonally but only if the numbers match.

Can you find a winning path? Ready, Set, GO!

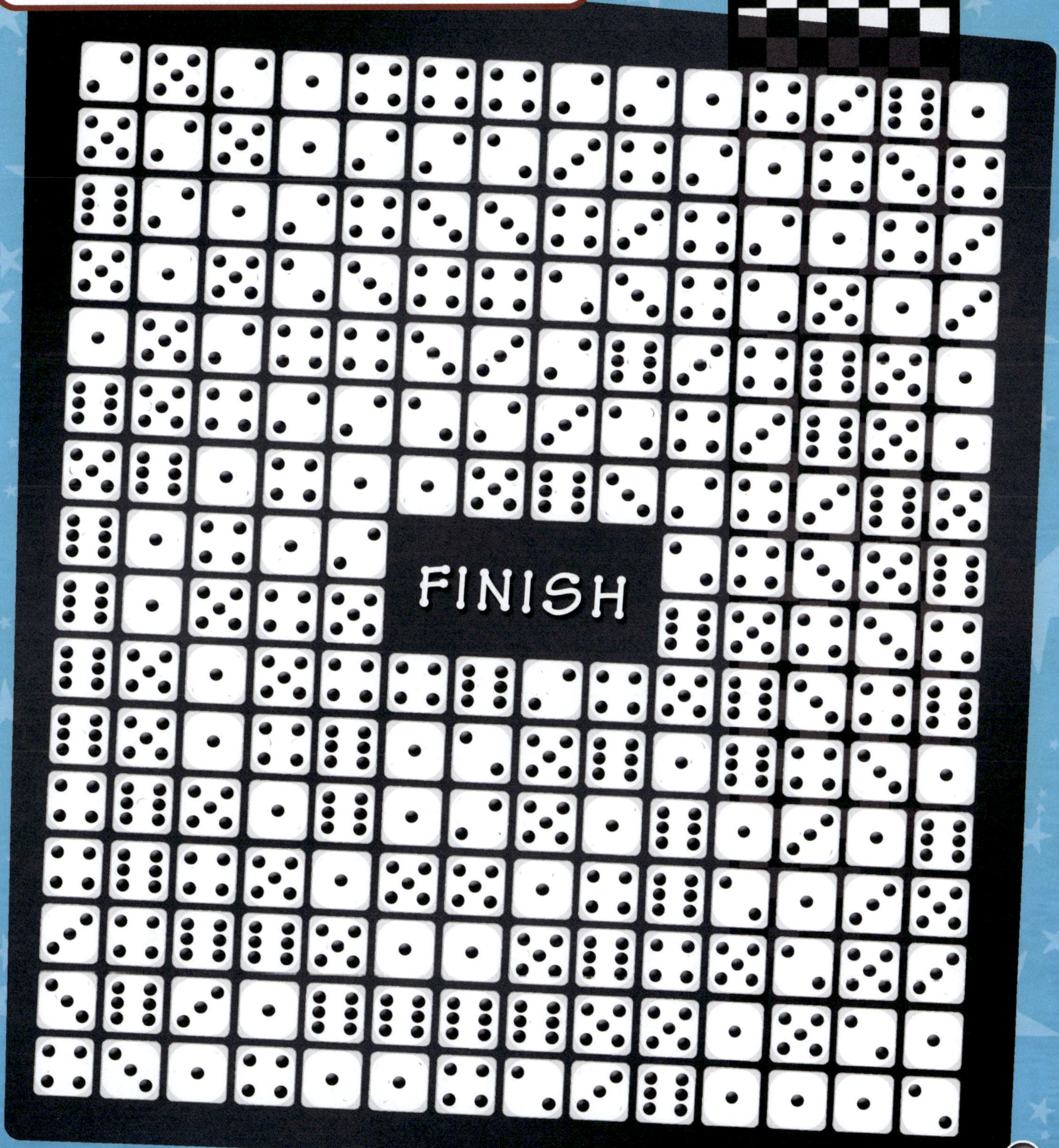

FINISH

A true magician
Howard Thurston

Born: July 20, 1869
Columbus, Ohio, USA

Background:

Howard Thurston was humble. He never bragged about what he could do and was always ready to listen and learn.

Famous Fact:

Thurston travelled all over the world and was known for being able to float a lady. Over 60 million people bought tickets to his show, but little did they know that when Thurston was a kid he was homeless and lived on the streets.

Quote: (Thurston said this before every show.)

"I am grateful because these people come to see me; they make it possible for me to make my living in a very agreeable way. I'm going to give them the very best I possibly can."

Howard Thurston
True Trait: Humble

Did you know?

Most decks have 52 cards and two jokers.

Seven shuffles of a deck of playing cards is all it takes to make it completly random.

Betcha...

Bet you I can make you say the word "brown."

Try it with a friend!

Start asking a friend the colors of various objects in the room, making sure that none of them are brown or blue. After four objects, ask, "What are the colors of the American flag?" When they respond, you say, "I win, I told you I could make you say 'blue'!" When they say, "You didn't say blue, you said brown." Then say, "You're right, now I win!"

S3CRET5

Card Shark

The Effect:
Always know which stack of cards will be selected.

The Secret:
You always write, "You will pick the 5 stack." Depending on how you display the cards, you will always be correct!

Materials:
A deck of cards, paper, and pen

Preparation:
Make two piles of cards, one with five cards in it (any five cards) and one with four cards in it. This pile should have the five of diamonds, five of clubs, five of spades, and five of hearts.

Presentation:
"Once I was swimming in the ocean and was bitten by a shark, but not just any shark, a card shark. Ever since that close encounter, I have had the ability to sense what someone will choose when it comes to cards. Come close, please place your hands over the cards and think of the stack you want." (Stare into their eyes.) "Oh I see...interesting." (Write down prediction.) "OK. Please pick up the stack that you want and then read my prediction."

Depending on which stack is chosen, tell the volunteer to either count the cards or turn them over. If they pick the stack with 5 cards, count them face down showing they chose the stack with 5 cards. If they pick the stack with the fives, turn both stacks over showing they chose the one with the fives.

SUPER Tic-Tac-Toe

Ask a friend to play this new game with you. It is the box game and tic tac toe combined!

Before making an "x" or "o" each player takes turns drawing a line connecting two dots either up and down or side to side. Complete a box and place your symbol inside, then it's the next players turn. Good luck!

Stare at the dot and slowly move this page towards your nose. Watch as the lady floats through the hoop!

Make an Optical Illusion

Connect the dots below and see what popular illusion you create.

Do you see three blocks or four?

Magic Jokes

Q: How many magicians does it take to change a light bulb?
A: It depends on what you want him to change it into!

Q: Why do magicians like tests?
A: Because they are really good at trick questions!

Q: If Houdini were alive today, what would he be famous for?
A: He'd be the oldest man alive!

Q: How much change does a mentalist carry in his pocket?
A: Six cents!

Q: Why don't ghosts make good magicians?
A: You can see through all their tricks!

Q: Why do wizards like school?
A: They are good at spelling!

Q: What do you call a magician on a plane?
A: A flying sorcerer!

Q: Did you hear about the Spanish magician?
A: He said "Uno, Dos" and then disappeared without a Tres!

Can you draw five straight lines so that each star is in its own box?
Hint: The five lines make a star.

Which Wand

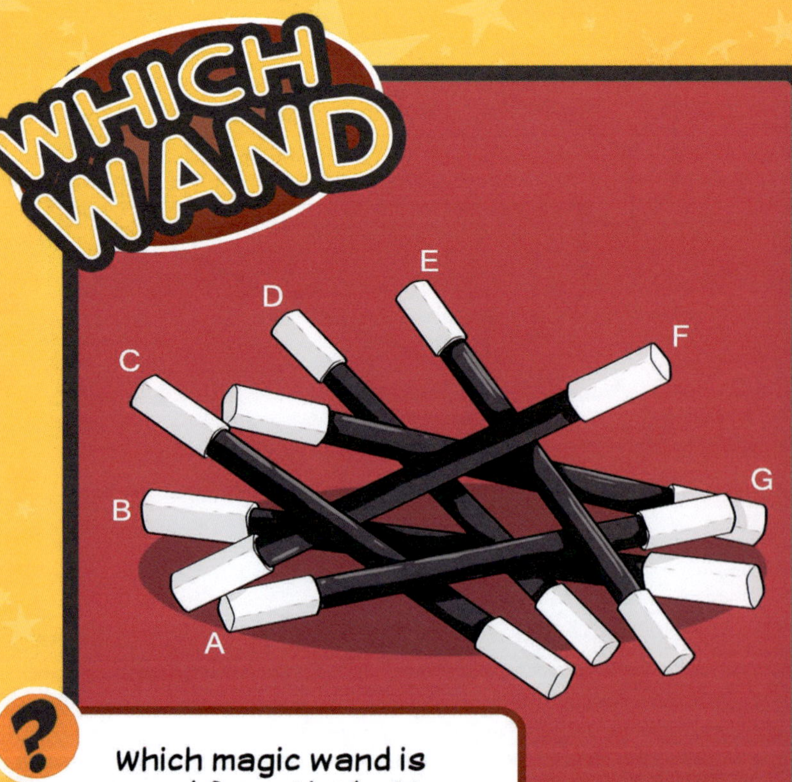

Which magic wand is second from the bottom of the stack?

THROUGH A BRICK WALL

Mr. Magic is going to do the famous magic trick "Walking through a brick wall."

Can you get from one side of the wall to the other?

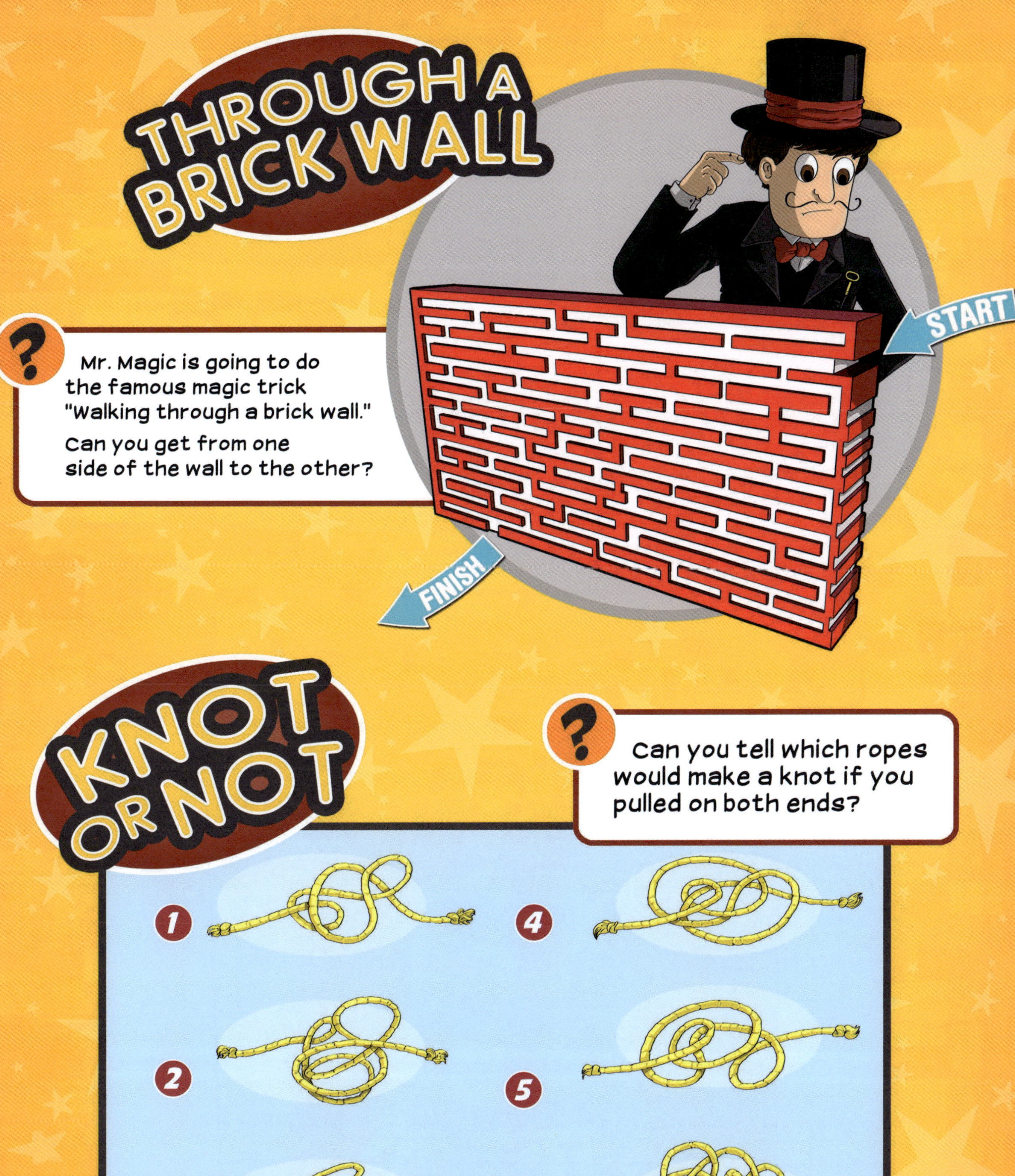

KNOT OR NOT

Can you tell which ropes would make a knot if you pulled on both ends?

WHERE IN THE WORLD

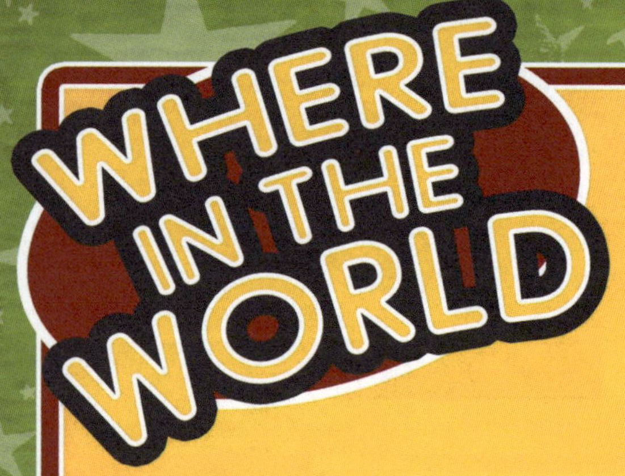

Can you find all the places Mr. Magic has taken his Show of Wonder? Look closely at his magic trunk for some clues.

A	U	F	J	V	P	O	A	I	S	R	D	G	X
U	I	Z	M	K	I	N	D	T	R	O	R	G	A
S	R	S	Q	Z	I	N	R	V	P	W	G	H	T
T	E	P	S	H	J	V	Z	X	E	J	X	F	O
R	L	A	C	C	C	F	Z	Q	C	E	F	B	Z
A	A	I	E	K	I	K	R	E	I	A	I	P	R
L	N	N	N	P	J	R	O	A	Q	R	M	T	P
I	D	B	G	T	B	A	L	C	N	B	O	B	D
A	I	U	L	S	R	P	N	M	I	C	G	C	Q
W	Z	S	A	I	A	V	F	P	I	L	E	A	O
T	C	K	N	T	Z	F	F	X	H	V	Y	F	Z
J	V	W	D	A	I	Q	E	D	S	F	T	O	C
K	F	P	N	L	L	M	C	A	N	A	D	A	Y
F	J	E	G	Y	P	T	D	S	Y	V	Q	Z	C

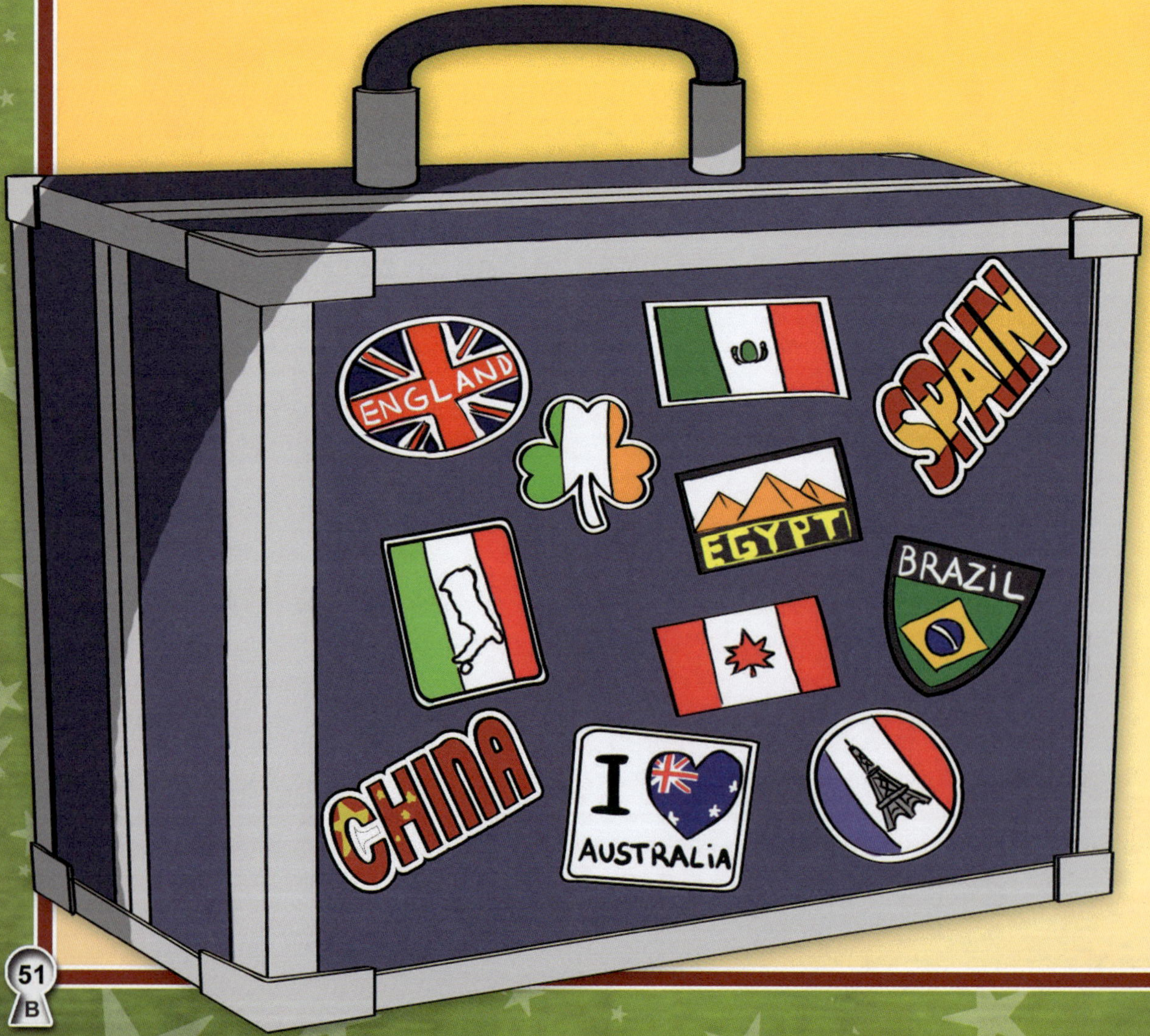

SMOKE AND MIRROR MAZE

START!

? Hold this page to a mirror upside down and you will see the start and the finish magically change so you can do the maze backwards.

FINISH

A true magician
Mr. Electric

Born: April 1, 1925
Los Angeles, California, USA

Background:

Mr. Electric was authentic. He never pretended to be something he wasn't. His goal was always to entertain by being the best he could be.

Famous Fact:

Mr. Electric had the special ability to light a 1000-watt light bulb in his bare hands, make strings of lit light bulbs come from his mouth, and could produce a lighted chandelier. He even learned to ice skate so he could do his show on ice.

Quote:

"Be in love with life. Be in love with people. Be a people person. Every person is so different. These are treasures."

Mr. Electric - Marvyn Roy
True Trait: Authentic

Did you know?

Latex balloons come from rubber trees that grow in rain forests.

When a latex balloon is released outside, it can rise to an altitude of over five miles before it freezes and pops.

TOOTHPICK MORE

Find out how on page 79

Betcha...

Grab 9 toothpicks and set them up as shown here making three triangles.

Bet you can't move three toothpicks and make four triangles.

LEARN MAGIC

S3CRET5

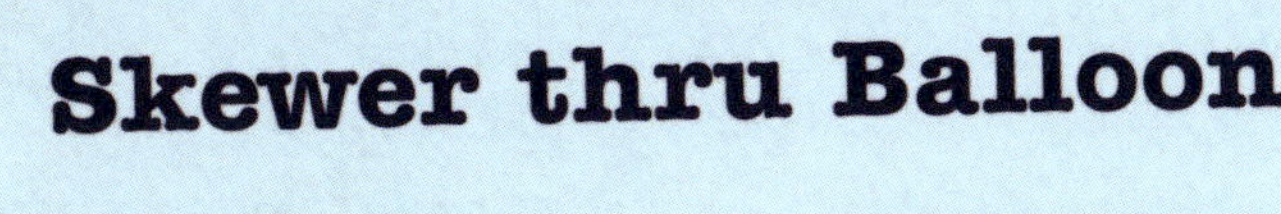

Skewer thru Balloon

The Effect:
Stick a wooden skewer through a balloon without it popping.

The Secret:
Petroleum jelly on the skewer makes it so that the skewer won't pop the balloon if you put it through the ends where the latex is darker and not as stretched out.

Materials:
Wooden skewer, large latex balloon, and petroleum jelly

Preparation:
Coat the wooden skewer with petroleum jelly.

Presentation:
"Have you ever heard of a magic hot air balloon? Here let me show you. (Pick up a deflated balloon) I have a balloon, I'll fill it with some hot air, which I have plenty. (Blow up the balloon and tie it. Do not over inflate the balloon. The more stretched out the balloon is, the weaker it will be.) And now the magic! (Pick up skewer) Watch as I bust through the balloon without a burst. (Carefuly insert the skewer near the mouth of the balloon where the latex is thicker and out through the top of the balloon if you wish.) Almost as if by magic—it won't pop. See? I wasn't full of hot air...or was I?"

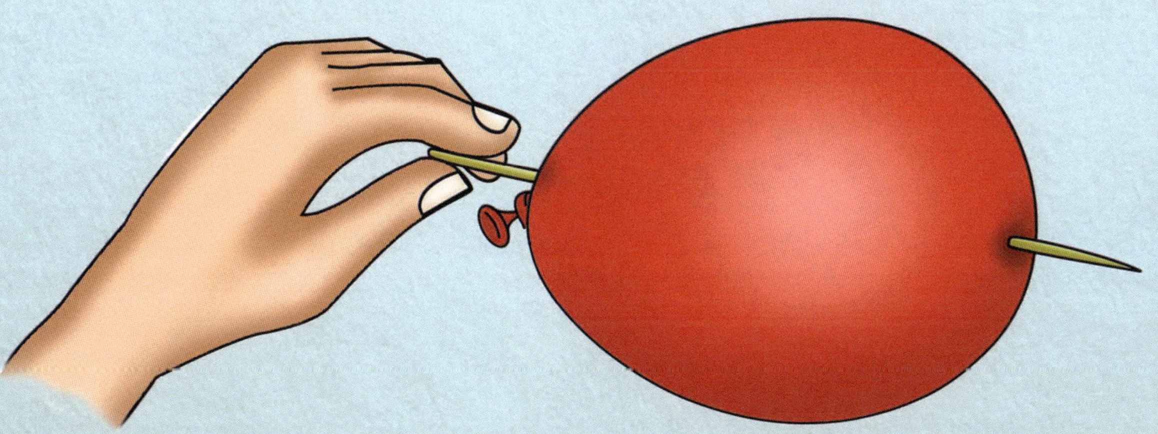

FANTASTIC BETCHAS

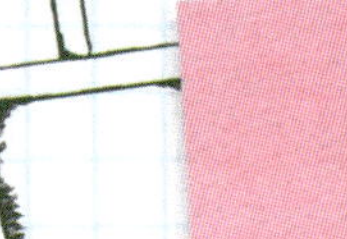

THE SECOND STRAW

"Bet you can't stick two drinking straws in your mouth and drink from a glass while one is outside of the glass."

Secret: The extra straw doesn't allow the suction needed to get the liquid out.

CRACK A SMILE

"Bet you can't eat eight saltine crackers one by one in 60 seconds without drinking anything."

Secret: The saltiness of the crackers gives most people "cotton mouth" so you can't eat more than five or six.

Which string can lift up the ice?

BREAK THE NOODLE

"Bet you can't break a piece of dry spaghetti into just two pieces by holding the ends."

Secret: No matter how hard you try, spaghetti won't break into just two pieces when holding both ends. TRY IT!

HANGING BY A THREAD

"Bet you can't lift an ice cube up without touching it."

Secret: Lay a piece of string across the top of the ice cube. Sprinkle some salt on the ice cube over the string. Wait 3 minutes and then carefully lift the string and the cube!

BIZARRE BOWLING

Which line is longer the red or the green?

Which ball is bigger the blue or the purple?

Which tile is darker tile "A" or tile "B"?

Believe it or not the red line and green line are the same length.
The blue bowling ball and the purple ball are the same size.
And tile "A" and tile "B" are the exact same color.

SHOW TIME
start
T
I
D
E
E
T
N
A

A race against the clock!

Can you help Mr. Magic get to his show on time? Fill in the letters that you cross to solve this riddle:

WHY DIDN'T THE CLOCK WORK?

ANSWER: __ ______ _ ____!

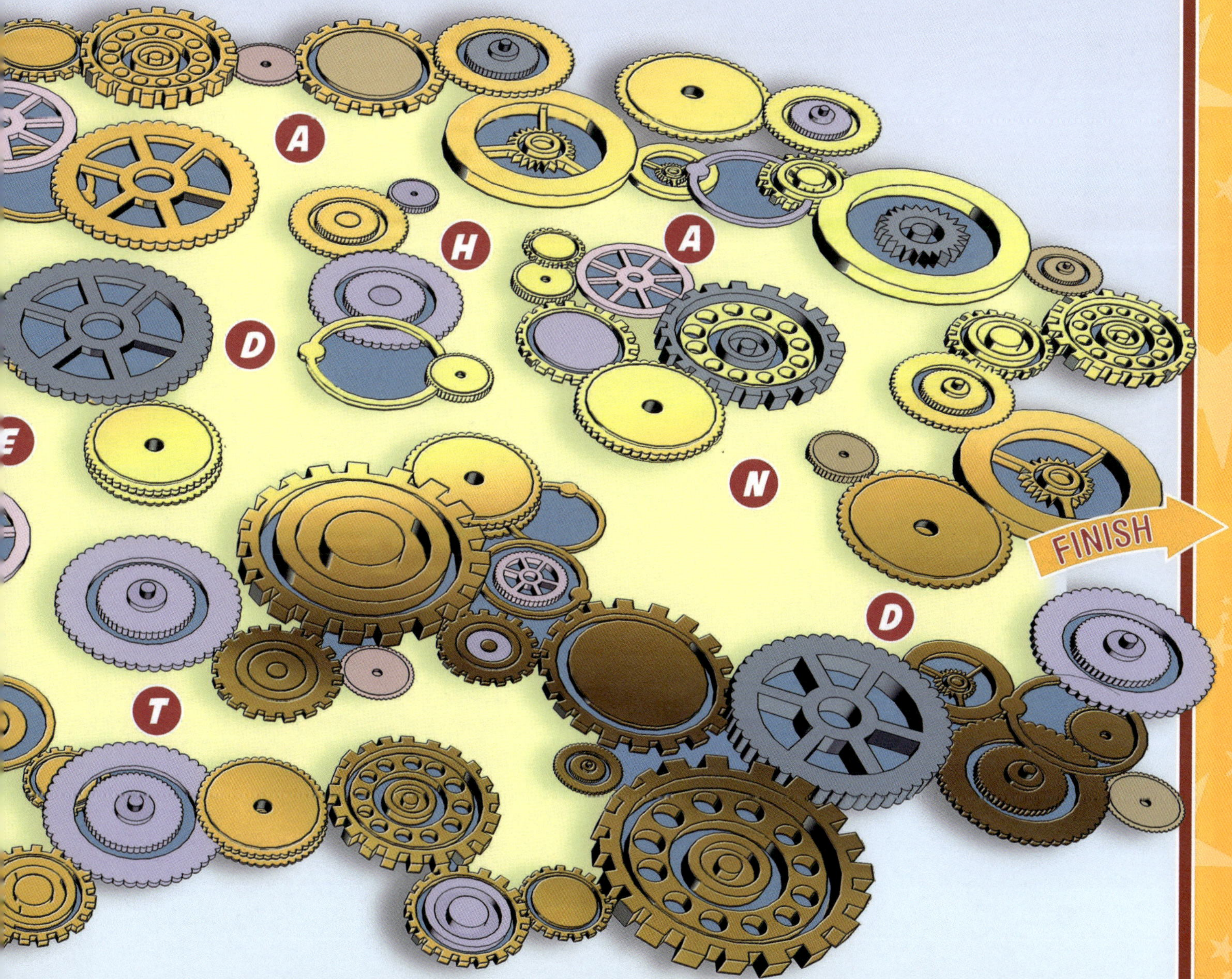

A H A D E N D T D

FINISH

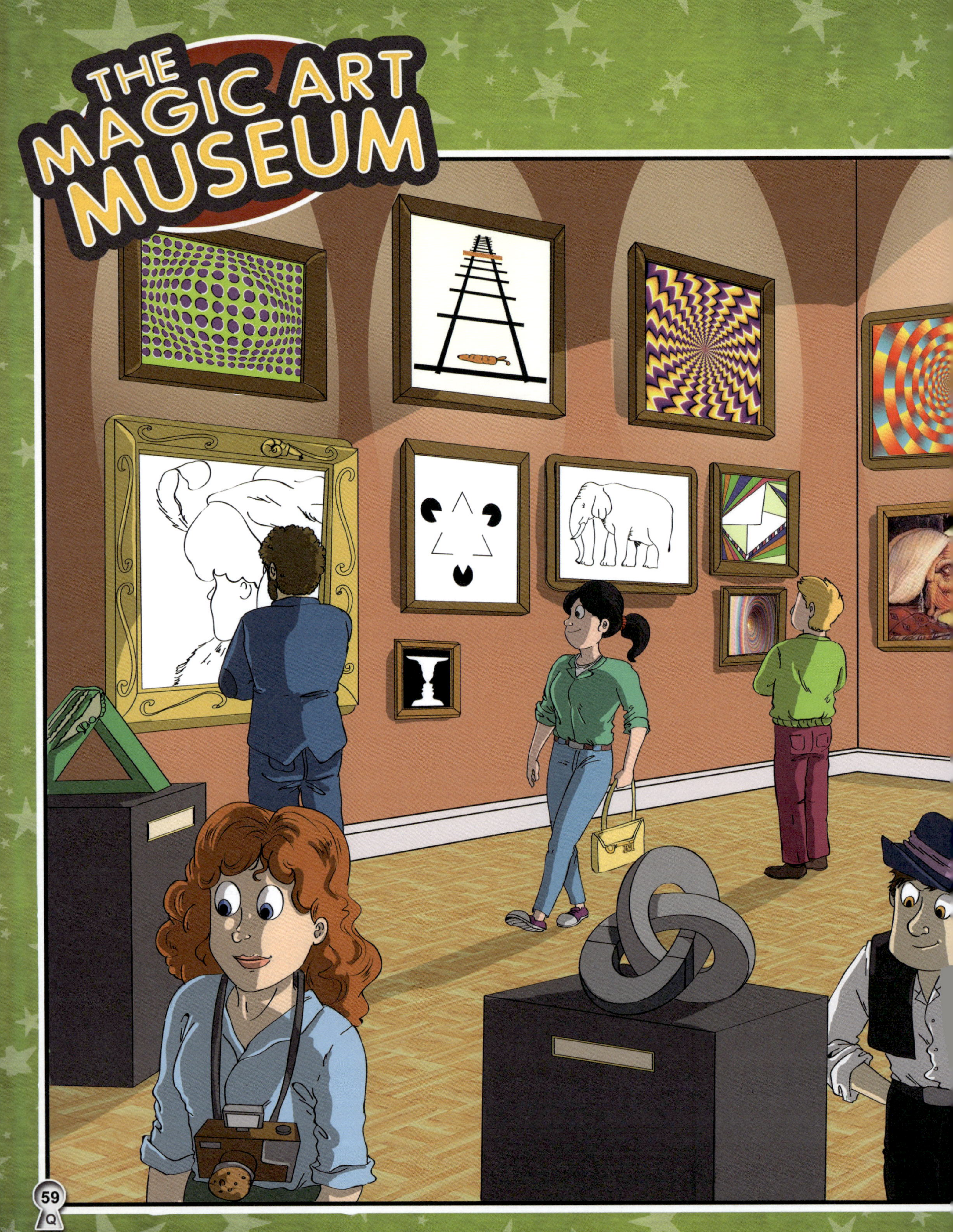
THE MAGIC ART MUSEUM

Not everything is what it seems to be in the art museum. Can you find all the hidden items?

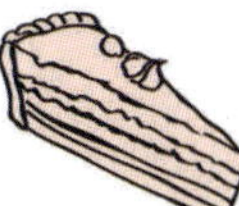
Cake slice

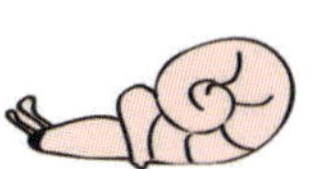
Snail

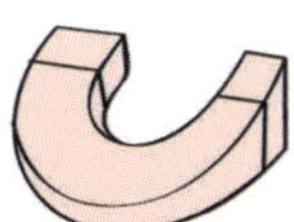
Magnet

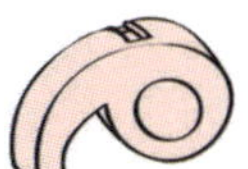
Whistle

Carrot

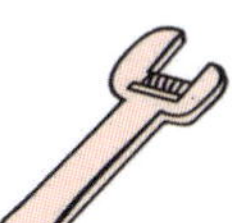
Wrench

Key

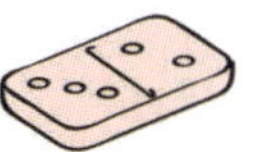
Domino

Cookie

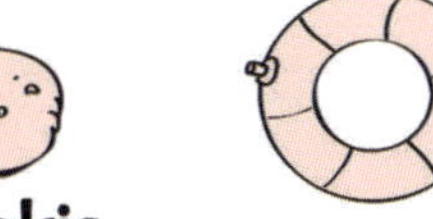
Lifesaver

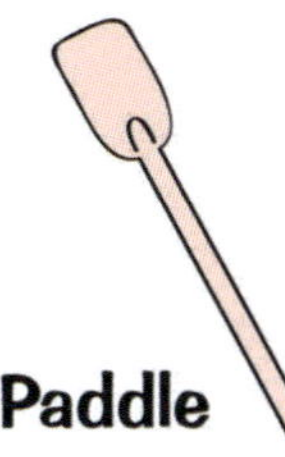
Paddle

Kite

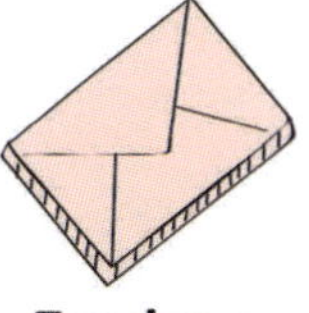
Envelope

Ruler

WHAT'S WRONG
You're in for a treat as you look for the 10 strange things that are in this silly picture.
1 TON
CONCESSION STAND
DRINKS

EASY

N	U	T	S
		N	
	S	U	
			T

MEDIUM

N	A	C	H	O	S
	H	O		C	N
	N				A
H	C		S		
		N	O	A	H
A	O			S	

HARD

S	O	F	T	D	R	I	N	K
I		N					D	
	R	D		I			O	F
F		S			K			D
T		R	I				K	
	K		D		S	F		
R		I	K	S			F	O
O			F		D			I
D		T	R			K	S	N

? SUDOKU

Each of these grids contains an item from the concession stand. Can you fill in the boxes so that each ROW, each COLUMN, and each BOX contains all the letters of the same snack?

A true magician
De Kolta

Born: November 18, 1847
Lyon, France, Europe

Background:

Buatier de Kolta was creative. He came up with his own ideas, wasn't afraid to fail or be different, and he always added his personal touch.

Famous Fact:

De Kolta was the creator of many magical illusions that are still used today, including Multiplying Billiard Balls, Spring Flowers, Vanishing Bird Cage, and was best known for the De Kolta Chair, which could make any lady vanish that sat on it.

Quote:

"An illusionist should never tell the public what he is going to do. If people know what is coming, they will not be surprised."

Buatier de Kolta
True Trait: Creative

Did you know?

People used to use their thumb, arm, or foot to measure things.

Then the inventor Eli Whitney had the idea of interchangeable parts and that created the need for stricter measurements.

This was the beginning of the modern day units.

CHANGE IS GOOD

Find out how on page 79

Betcha...

Get eight coins and place them on the table as shown here. This makes four rows of three coins.

Bet you can't move one coin so that you have six rows of three coins each.

S3CRET5

Appearing Ruler

The Effect:
Pull a ruler or other long skinny object out of a small envelope.

The Secret:
The ruler is hidden behind your arm held by a watch or bracelet. You just pretend to pull the ruler out from the envelope, really it comes from behind.

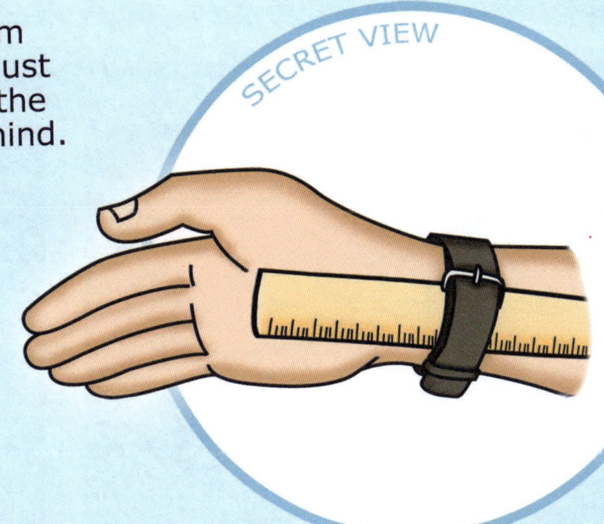

Materials:
A small envelope, a watch or bracelet, and a ruler or other object bigger than the envelope (like a paintbrush or magic wand)

Preparation:
Fold the envelope in half (so it is even smaller).

Place the ruler behind your arm held in place by your watch band or bracelet.

Presentation:
"Here I have one of the newest envelopes the post office is using. It's called the-fit-anything envelope. Let's see what is inside... this one my friend just sent me. (Open envelope and take out ruler.) Only problem is, once you take it out you can't put it back in, which isn't really measuring up to people's expectations..."

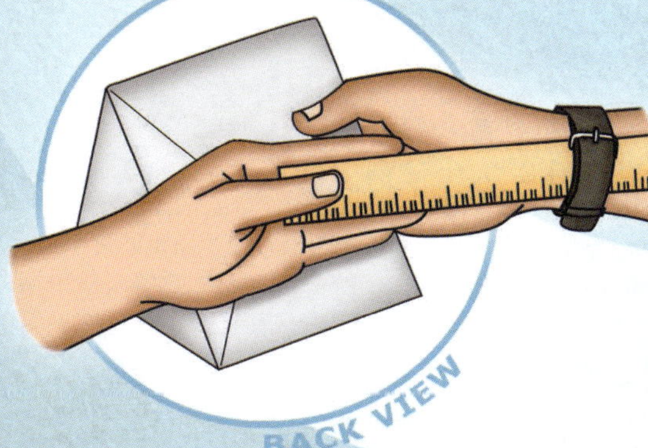

Not everything reflects in Mr. Magic's mirror.

Can you find all TEN items that are missing in the second image?

Mr. Magic left his rabbit cage open and all 26 of his rabbits got loose.

Can you find each of them in this word find? Words go up down and diagonal.

Apricot
Betsy
Cocoa
Dunkin
Edwin
Fanny
Geronimo
Harold
Icarus
Jack
Kermit
Larry
Moxie
Nincompoop
Orion
Puga
Quincy
Roxy
Stew
Thunder
Ulysses
Violet
Wiggles
Xray
Yogi
Zelda

A	R	K	E	R	M	I	T	B	E	D	W	I	N	N
J	D	H	C	O	C	O	A	F	E	M	D	E	R	I
A	H	A	M	Z	V	I	O	L	E	T	E	G	U	N
C	E	R	K	E	N	H	P	U	G	A	S	D	L	C
K	F	O	M	U	T	H	U	N	D	E	R	Y	Y	O
A	N	L	G	E	R	O	N	I	M	O	V	H	S	M
N	P	D	R	F	M	O	X	I	E	D	S	X	S	P
B	Y	R	L	E	Q	Q	G	P	E	V	N	R	E	O
I	X	O	I	N	E	U	P	D	O	I	F	A	S	O
L	C	V	G	C	X	F	I	O	K	O	M	Y	M	P
Z	A	A	G	I	O	L	A	N	K	O	R	M	I	X
E	Y	R	R	P	N	T	U	N	C	D	S	I	G	P
L	M	N	R	U	S	D	Q	W	N	Y	M	Q	O	Y
D	P	T	N	Y	S	T	E	W	V	Y	J	Q	Q	N
A	J	R	O	X	Y	K	C	W	I	G	G	L	E	S

Can you find the two rabbits that look exactly alike?

Grab a friend and take turns placing your pen at the start of the spell (the blue dot). Close your eyes and try to draw a line to the end (the yellow dot) without hitting the sides.

See who can cast each spell in the least amount of strokes. NOTE: Each time you open your eyes it is a stroke. If your pen touches the sides that counts as two strokes. Good Luck!!!

Levitating Taco

Vanishing Little Sister

Walking through A brick wall
Turning A Frog into gold coins
Appearing Cupcake

Rabbit Jokes

Q: Did you hear about the angry magician?
A: He pulled his hare out!

Q: How do you know carrots are good for your eyes?
A: Because you never see a rabbit wearing glasses!

Q: What did the rabbit give his girlfriend?
A: A 24 carrot ring!

Q: What did the rabbit say to the carrot?
A: It's been nice gnawing you!

Q: What's a rabbit's favorite game?
A: Hopscotch!

Q: What is a rabbit's favorite dance style?
A: Hip-Hop!

Q: What do you call a rabbit comedian?
A: A funny bunny!

Q: What did the bunny say to the duck?
A: You quack me up!

Can you find the one note that is different?

Can you find all eight traits of a true magician in this word search?

```
T H C B M F D R G
E A O Y R C W R I
N U N Q V C V E V
T T F V H R C S I
H H I H U E D P N
U E D P M G O E G
S N E R B T N C X
I T N E L I O T L
A I T P E V B F V
S C B A P E B U Y
T K B R O K L L B
I C R E A T I V E
C J O D P U R B M
```

A True Magician is...

- RESPECTFUL
- PREPARED
- ENTHUSIASTIC
- CONFIDENT
- HUMBLE
- CREATIVE
- AUTHENTIC
- GIVING

12
ABC
14

Do you see "13" or "B"?

PICTURE PIECES

This piece of art is called "White Tiger in a snowstorm in China."

If you had to color each piece so that no two adjoining pieces are the same color. What is the minimum number of colors you would need?

A true magician
Blackstone Sr.

Born: September 27, 1885
Chicago, Illinois, USA

Background:

Harry Blackstone Sr. was **giving**. He gave without expecting anything in return. Knowing that the real gift was the feeling the audience would get, Blackstone created memories that would last forever.

Famous Fact:

During each of his magic shows, Harry would make a bunny and chocolates appear. He would give the bunny to a child in the audience as a gift and the box of chocolates was for the mother.

Quote:

"The personality must be bigger than the prop."

Harry Blackstone Sr.
True Trait: Giving

Did you know?

Sugar is the main ingredient in rocket fuel used by amateur rocket enthusiasts.

Eating too much sugar can result in a loss of memory.

MIXING SALT & PEPPER

Betcha...

Pour salt and pepper onto a plate and mix them. Bet you can't separate all the pepper from the salt.

Secret: Blow up a balloon and rub it on your shirt for a static charge. When placing it over the salt and pepper, the pepper will jump to the balloon leaving just the salt.

LEARN MAGIC

S3CRET5

Vanishing Sugar

The Effect:
Make sugar disappear in your hand.

The Secret:
You never really put sugar in your hand, you only pretend to with a specially prepared sugar packet.

Materials:
Several small packets of sugar

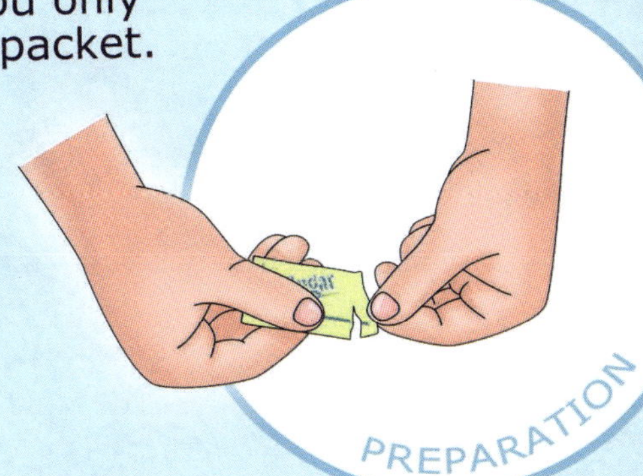

Preparation:

1. Carefully tear a sugar packet open on one end.
2. Pour out almost all of the sugar.
3. Fold the torn edge back down so it looks like an unopened sugar packet.

Presentation:

"Did you know sugar is magic? It makes everything sweet and once it is poured into something it becomes invisible. Seriously you can't see it but you know it's in there! Here let me show you. I will take this sugar..."

Grab your prepared packet and flick it making it sound like sugar is inside. Rip it open. Make a fist and pretend to pour it into your hand letting the last few pieces fall on top of your fist. Wipe those away giving the impression that everything has been poured in.

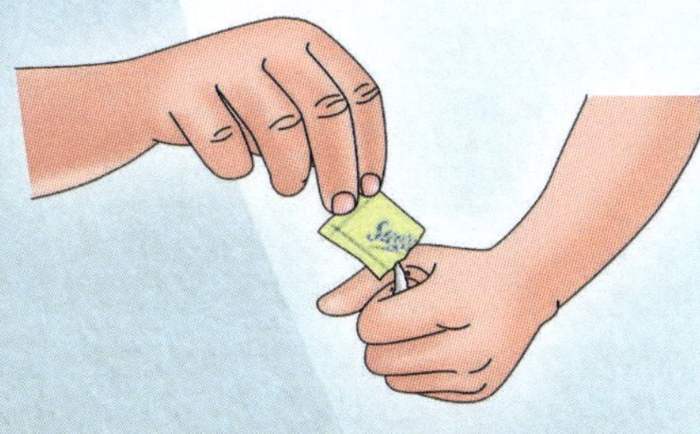

"...Pour it into my hand and say the magic word 'sweet tooth.'" Wave your hand over your fist and then slowly open your fist to reveal the sugar has vanished.

"Now isn't that sweet?"

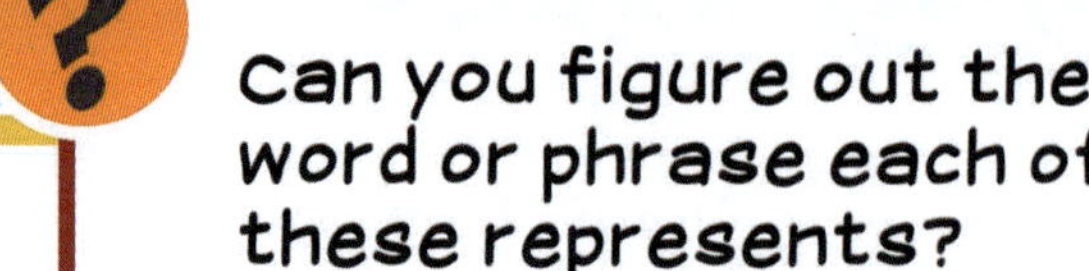

SPORTS

RETRAUQ

Juggling Side show!

Look at this picture for 30 seconds. Memorize as much as you can, then turn the page and see how much you can remember.

SIDESHOW

Juggling Side Show Quiz!

(From previous page)

1. How many hats are there?
2. What animal is on a barrel?
3. What color are the flags?
4. What animal is juggling rings?
5. What does the sign on the stage say?
6. How many animals are there?
7. How many balls are there?
8. What color are the stairs?

TEN TONGUE TWISTERS

1. I saw Esau sitting on a seesaw. Esau, he saw me.
2. The instinct of an extinct insect stinks.
3. Magic Maggie makes metal marbles magnetic.  
4. Whirly waves of Wally's white wand.
5. Silly Sam shaved seven shy sheep.
6. What noise annoys a noisy oyster? A noisy noise annoys a noisy oyster!
7. Double bubblegum bubbles double.
8. My sister's shop sells shoes for sheep.
9. Purple puzzle pieces Peter put perfect.
10. Looks like Luke's luck lasted long.

SHEEP SHOE SH

VANISHING CARS

Make all the cars disappear (Cross out the word car wherever you see it) and the remaining letters will give you the answer to this silly riddle.

A C A R G A C
C A R C A R A
R C A R B A R
G E C A R T R
C C U C A R C
A A C A R C A
R R K C A R R

WHAT HAS FOUR WHEELS AND FLIES?

MATCHING HATS

Each hat has a perfect match except for one.

Can you find the one that doesn't fit?

TRUE MAGICIANS

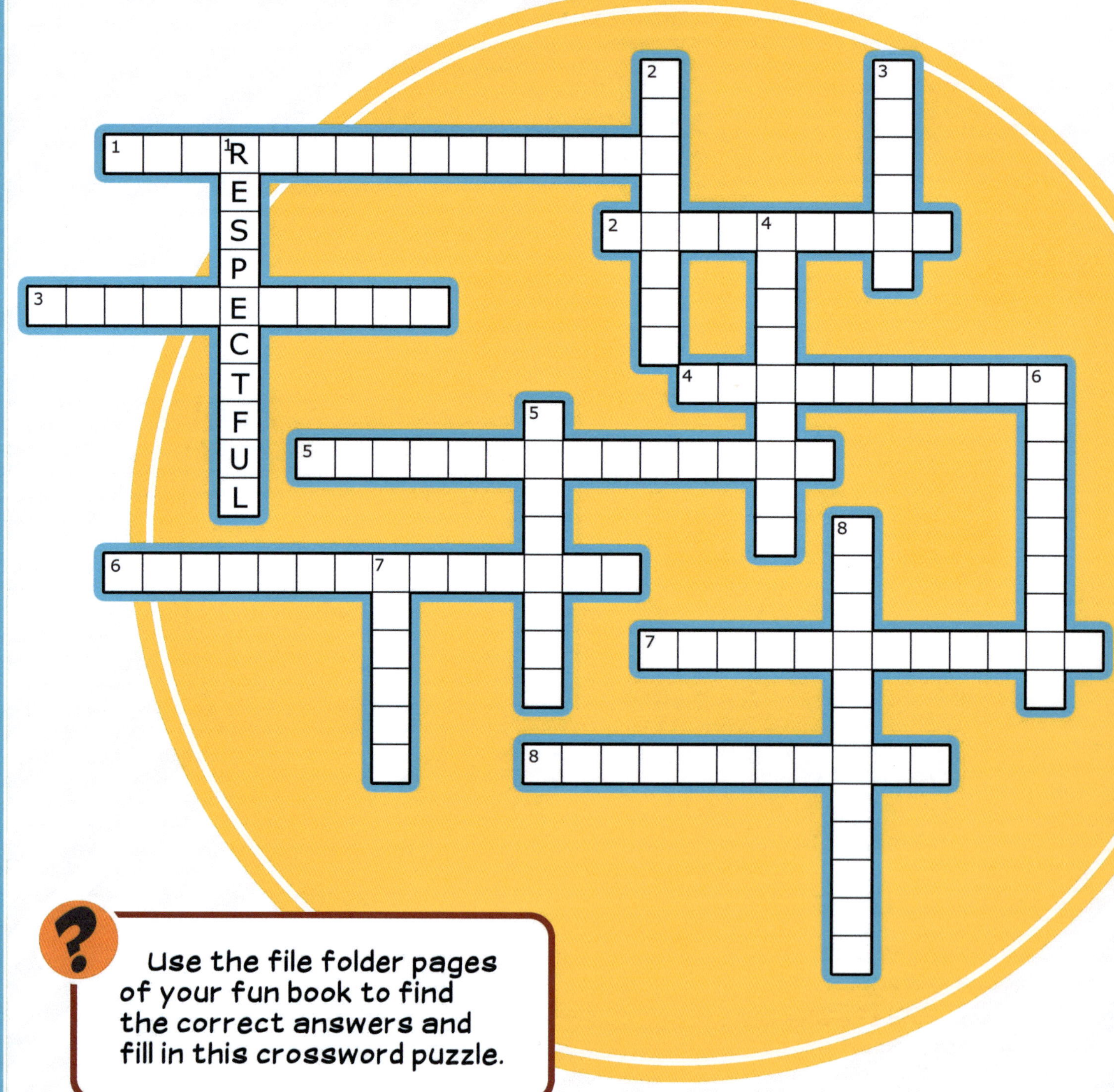

Use the file folder pages of your fun book to find the correct answers and fill in this crossword puzzle.

ACROSS:
(Magicians)

1. Gave bunnies to kids
2. Had small hands
3. Made others shine
4. Did magic shows on ice
5. Born in France
6. Famous for floating a lady
7. Greatest escape artist
8. Used bright colors

DOWN:
(True Traits)

1. Treating others fairly
2. Always ready
3. Serving freely
4. True to yourself
5. Using your own ideas
6. Knowing you can
7. Never bragging
8. Being positive

DiscoverMagic.com/ H _ _ _ _ _ _
72 56 36 5 46 13 39

Visit this secret web page to learn even more magic. Use the page numbers to decode the address.

CHANGE IS GOOD

DON'T TIP THE BOTTLE

TOOTHPICK MORE

TOOTHPICK BOXES

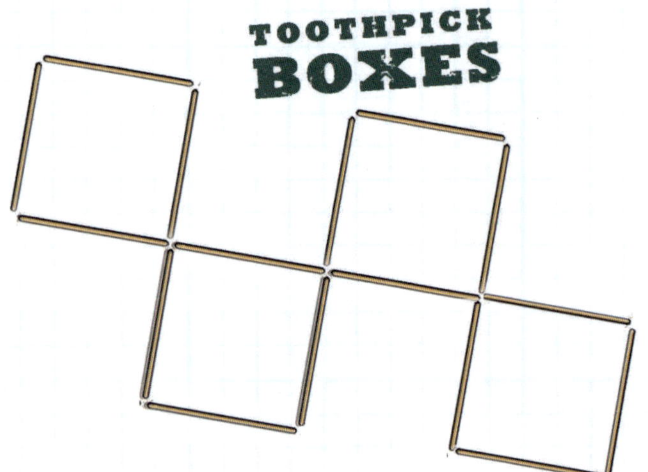

MAKING THE CHANGE

ANSWERS

1 The Magic Shop

3 Chain Escape

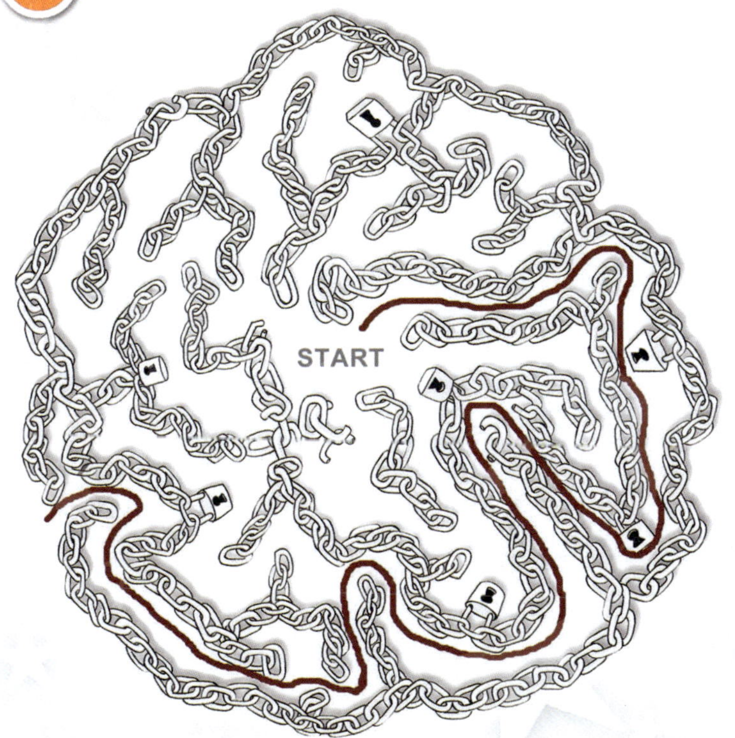

4 Magic Word Search

U I A B Z Z T W L L L I K E S P R C C H
O F F Y Y D Y R J P T N E B F H N J Z O
B O M E D L S G V O L R Y B E W D B G C
V R O J R H D T M Z Q S A M K D V J H U
M G U C N M F R I P C H A L N Q Y H N S
Y I M Z R Q A N V N L S M P A Y K S J P
G V F I V S N H U J E E K R U K L L W O
M E D T N F J O Q S J M A E R S A D O C
P Y I V B O Y N N U O W Y S K H R Z M U
G O J G L K A E J X Z G Z T E A M B A S
G U I L N E P F J R C K I O U Z B V N M
E G E A O O J D D O W T S C M A G I C S
S H H X V A I M S O R R Y H A M A A K K
F T H A B R A C A D A B R A K N Z F B D
O Q B U I U N D E R S T A N D D E J K L
G R E A T J O B U C P X N G G X A I A O
Q Q L X W I C Z E L D Z N O T V F G E V
E K K X O H T F S I M S A L A B I M O P

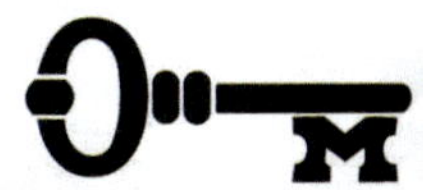

ANSWERS

5 Mind Reading

1. Smile
2. Chicken
3. Pizza
4. Magic
5. Spoon
6. Pencil
7. Candy
8. Lizard
9. Hamster

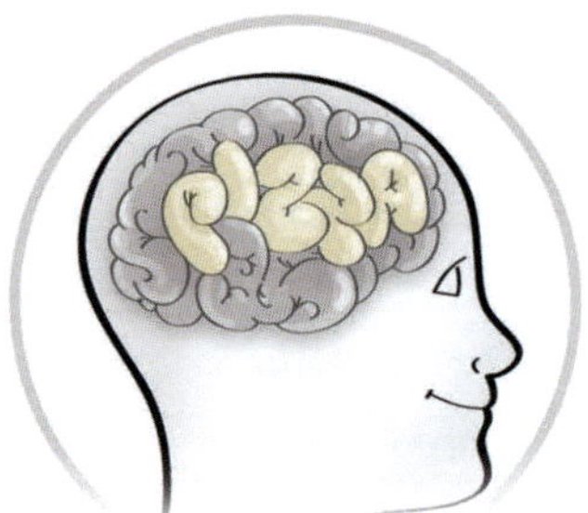

11 Picture Riddles

7 Dots Possible

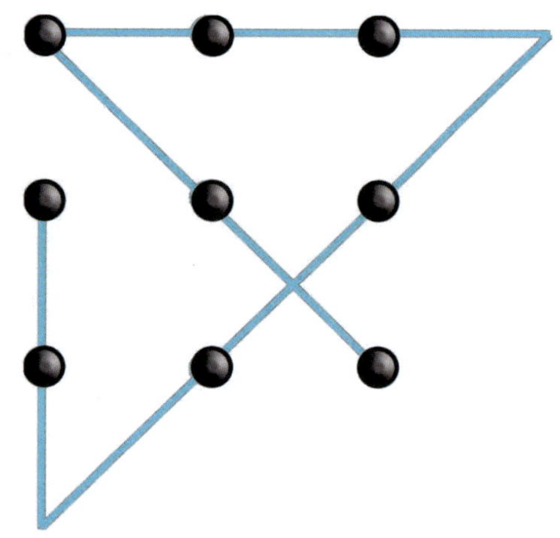

12 Appearing Animals

1. Giraffe
2. Raccoon
3. Hippopotamus
4. Elephant
5. Zebra
6. Tiger
7. Monkey
8. Alligator
9. Snake
10. Rabbit
11. Hamster
12. Mouse
13. Whale
14. Turtle
15. Dolphin
16. Donkey
17. Crocodile
18. Flamingo
19. Sheep
20. Turkey
21. Penguin
22. Skunk

8 Connect The Dots

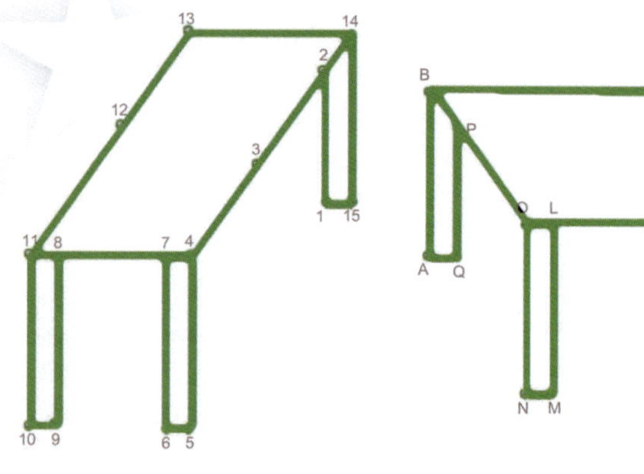

13 Magic Quote

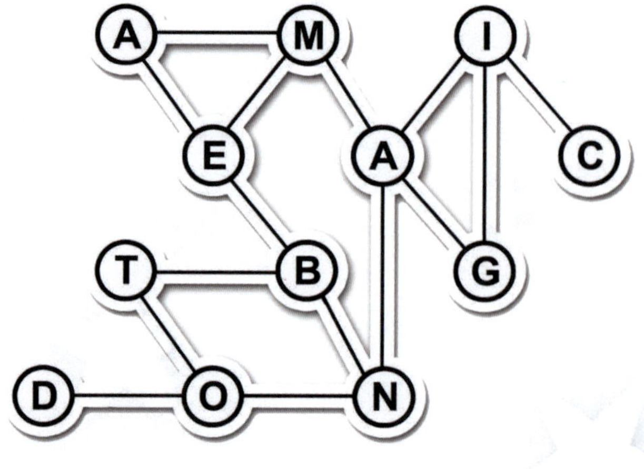

DO NOT BE A MAGICIAN
BE MAGIC!
- Leonard Cohen

ANSWERS

14 Sawing A Lady

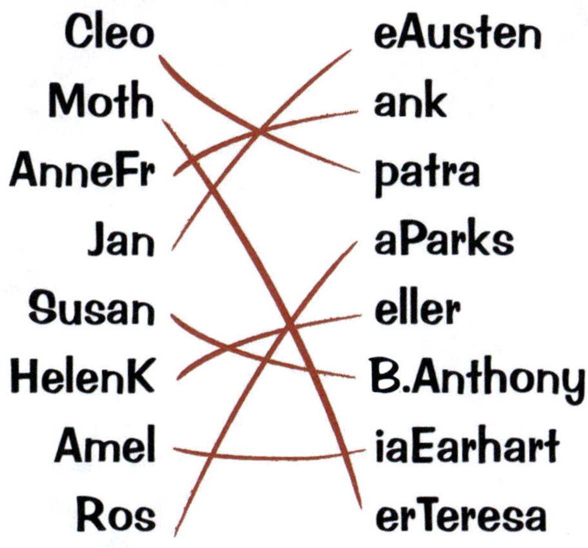

15 Secret Words

1. Handle with care
2. Fill in the blank
3. Right between the eyes
4. Feeling under the weather
5. Think outside the box
6. Amaze

7. Hotdog
8. Scrambled eggs
9. Banana split
10. Pancake
11. Club sandwich
12. Pasta salad

16 The Magic Show

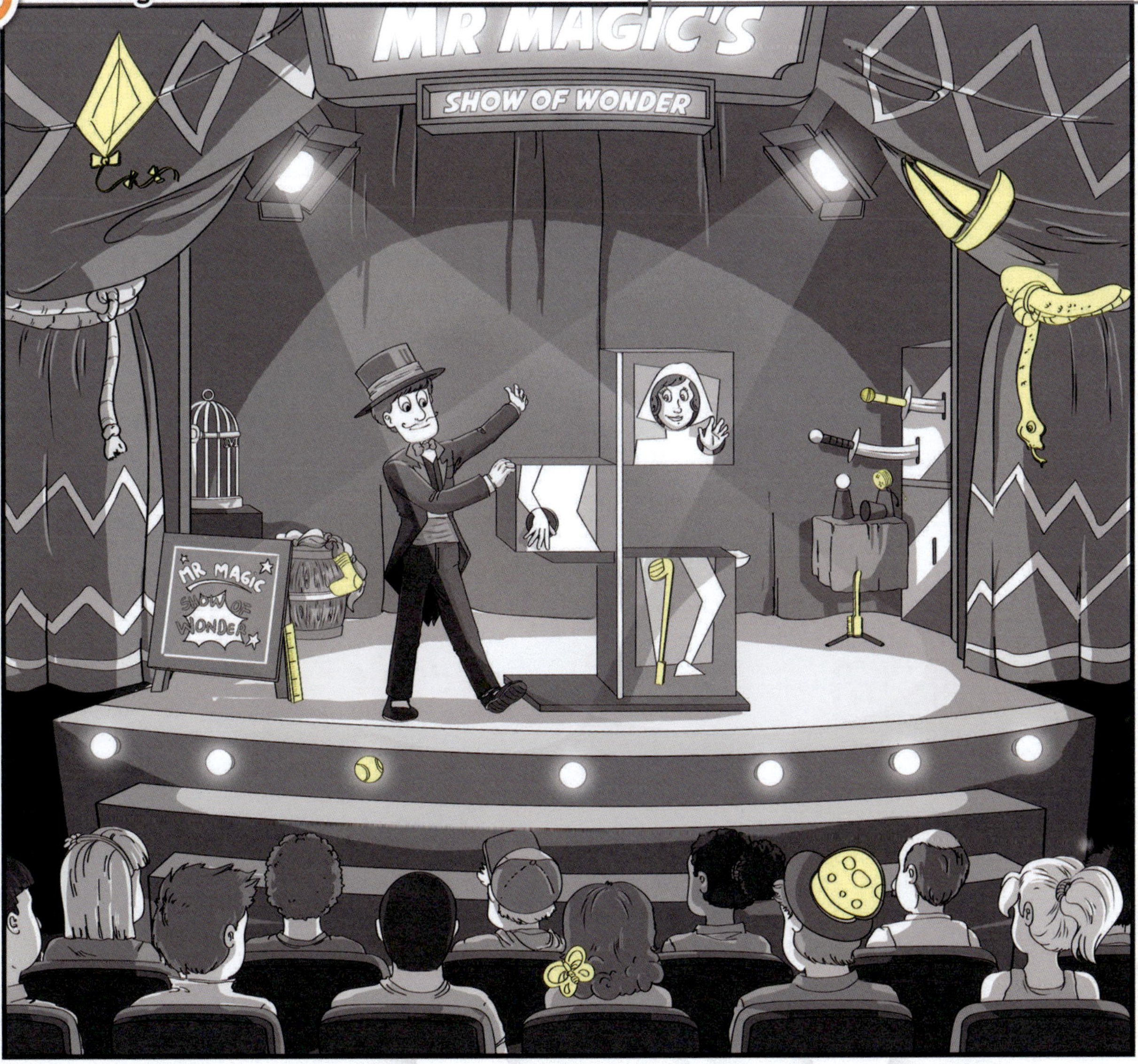

MR MAGIC'S

SHOW OF WONDER

ANSWERS

19 Linking Words

DOWN

1. Peanut Butter Knife
2. Trash Can Opener
3. Magic Book Worm
4. Pepperoni Pizza Party
5. Tree Top Hat
6. Horse Shoe Lace
7. Pig Pen Pal
8. Revolving Door Bell
9. Arm Pit Stop
10. Cotton Candy Apple
11. Bottled Water Melon
12. Cannon Ball Game

ACROSS

1. Hot Air Balloon Animal
2. Copy Cat Fish
3. Shark Tooth Paste
4. Toilet Paper Airplane
5. Mouse Trap Door
6. Vanilla Ice cream Truck
7. Piano Key Chain
8. Corn Dog House
9. Rail Road Runner

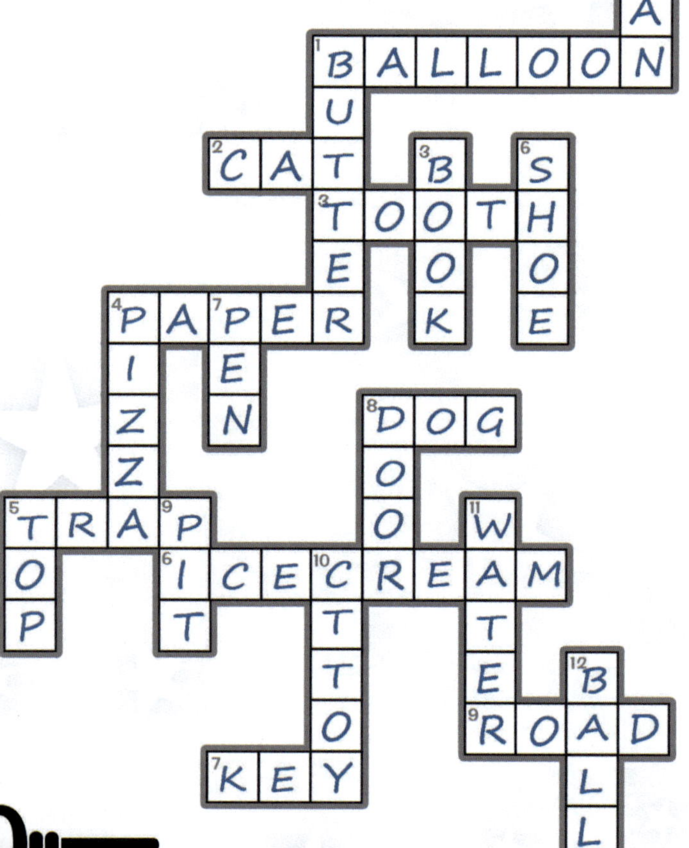

21 Miss-Tree Forest Quiz

1. Squirrels
2. A Doughnut
3. Brown
4. Three
5. None
6. White
7. Yellow
8 Seven

22 Acrobatic Jack Maze

22 Cube Puzzle

ANSWERS

23 Back Stage

25 Bag Of Tricks

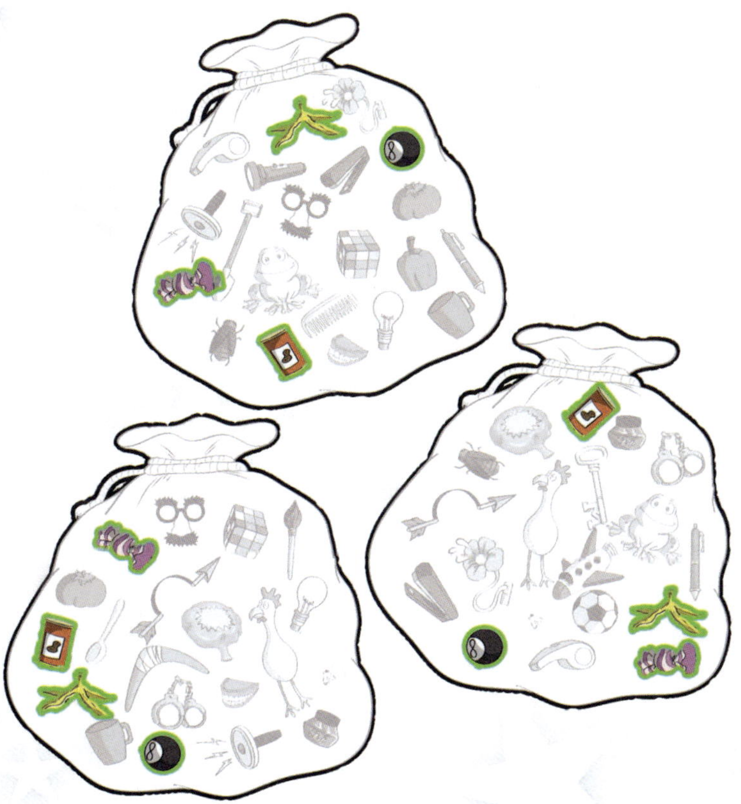

26 Crack The Code

ANASWER: A Computer Keyboard.

ANSWERS

29 Pair Of Jacks

30 8 Effects Of Magic

32 Lost In The Deck

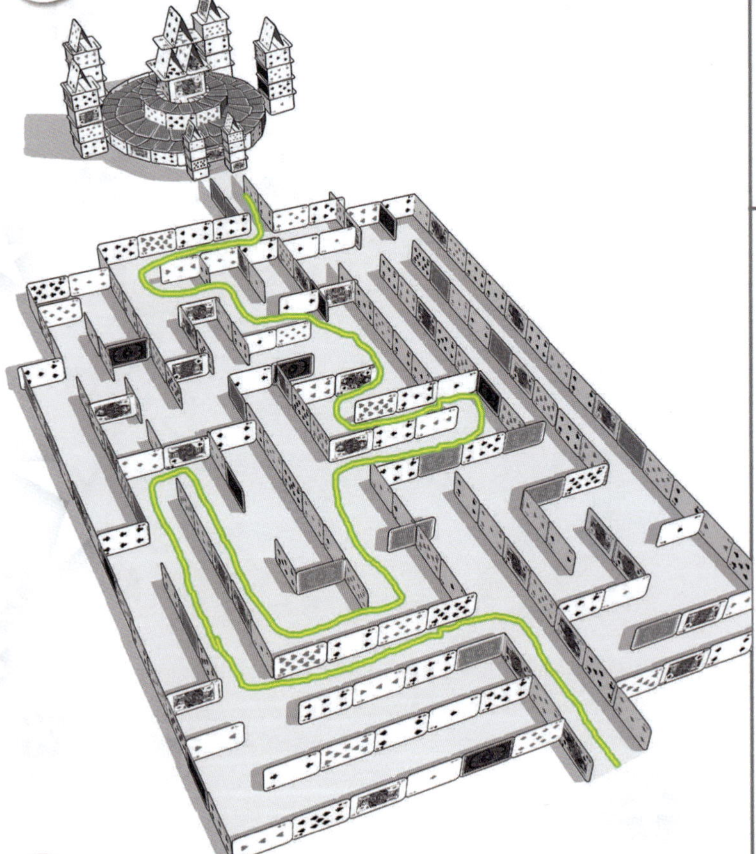

33 Mix And Match Riddles

1. Holes
2. The library
3. Your name
4. Short
5. Your fingernail
6. A shadow
7. Time
8. Nothing
9. A smile
10. Your breath
11. Silence
12. Your word

34 Terrific Ticket

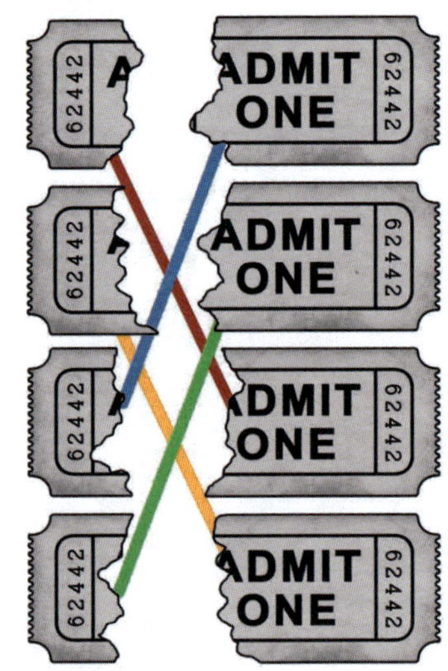

34 Cups And Balls

W X F B P H I C C U P N Z
S K B A L L E R I N A O S
N O F C G U M B A L L C S
O C G R T E A C U P T C Y
W C U P I D S F L R R U X
B U T T E R C U P R B P B
A P C U P B O A R D Z A A
L I C U P C A K E C L T L
L E M E A T B A L L M I L
L D B B A L L R O O M O O
O L J R E Y E B A L L N O
G D V E R B A L L Y W V N

35 Future Number

3 5
1 0 8 9 4
7 0 6 1 2 4 1
4 9 8 1 0 8 9 0 7
3 2 9 1 8 1 0 8 9
7 1 0 8 9 0 3 9 8
2 3 1 0 8 9 6
1 0 8 9 2
4 1 0

36 Secret Words

1. Ready for anything
2. Half empty
3. Magic box
4. Breakfast
5. One in a million
6. Disappearing ink

7. Parakeets
8. Three blind mice
9. Queen bee
10. Monkey
11. School of fish
12. Daddy long legs

40 Shadow Puppets

41 Magic Squares

4	9	2
3	5	7
8	1	6

16	3	2	13
5	10	11	8
9	6	7	12
4	15	14	1

ANSWERS

42 Mind Reading

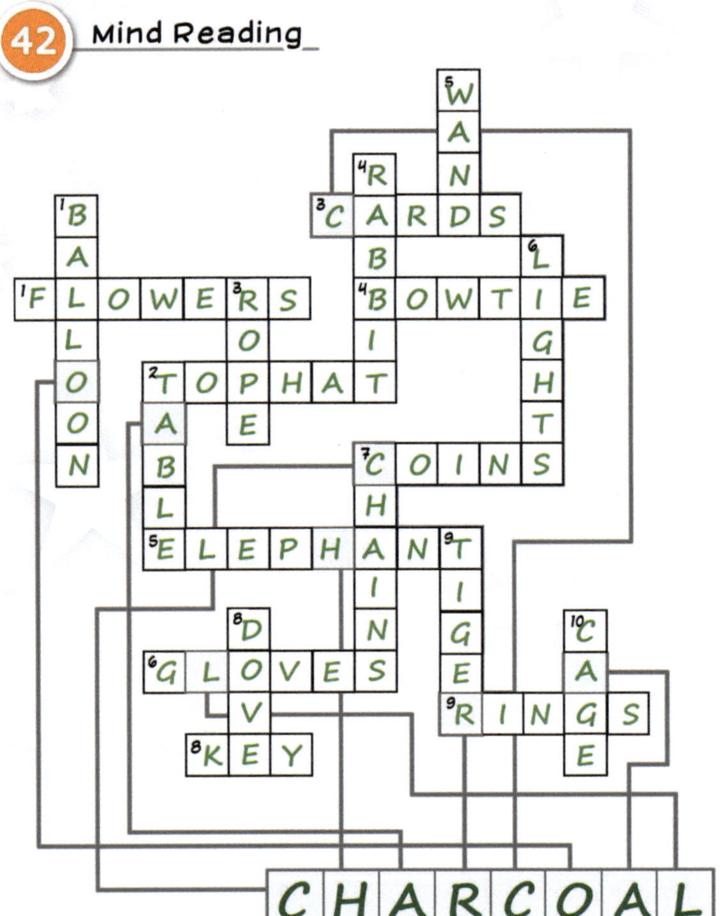

43 Shuffled Cards

G	I	F	T
F	T	G	I
I	G	T	F
T	F	I	G

T	H	A	N	K	Y	O	U
N	O	H	U	T	A	K	Y
Y	K	O	T	U	H	N	A
A	U	Y	K	N	O	H	T
K	A	N	Y	H	U	T	O
U	T	K	A	O	N	Y	H
O	N	U	H	Y	T	A	K
H	Y	T	O	A	K	U	N

43 Shuffled Cards

B	I	R	T	H	D	A	Y
D	H	A	Y	I	B	R	T
Y	A	D	B	T	R	H	I
R	T	H	I	Y	A	B	D
A	D	Y	H	R	T	I	B
T	R	I	A	B	Y	D	H
H	Y	B	D	A	I	T	R
I	B	T	R	D	H	Y	A

44 Dizzy Dice Dash

ANSWERS

48 Connect The Dots

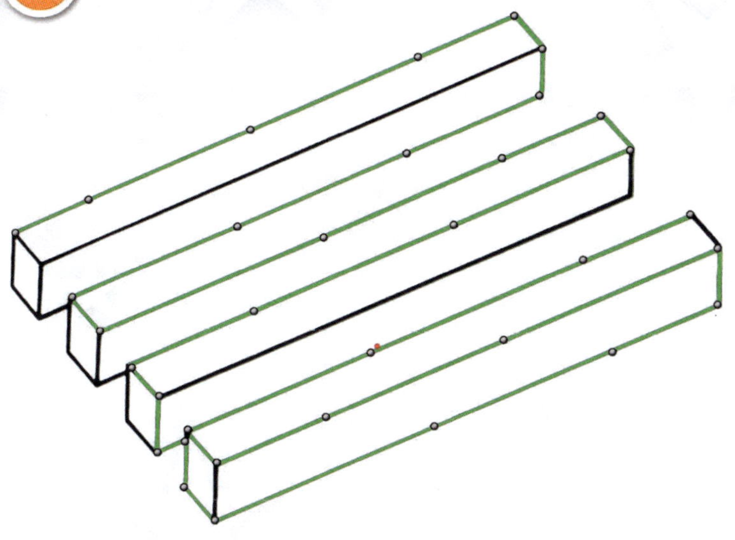

49 Star Burst

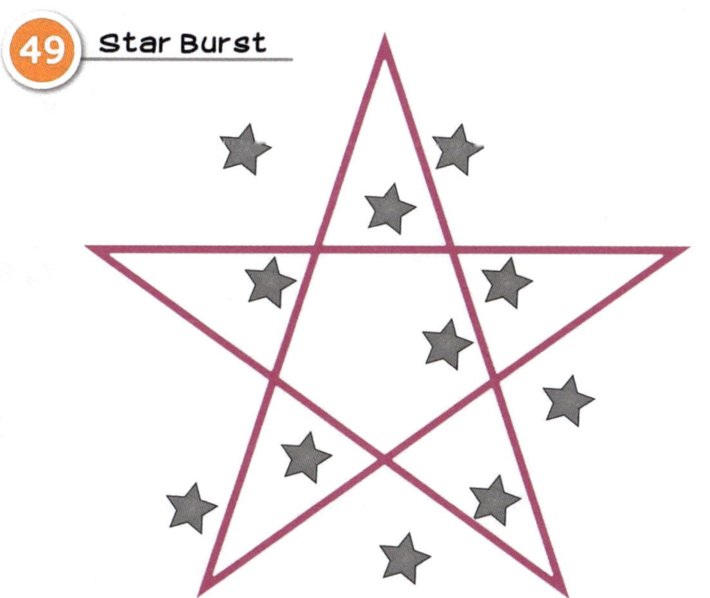

49 Which Wand

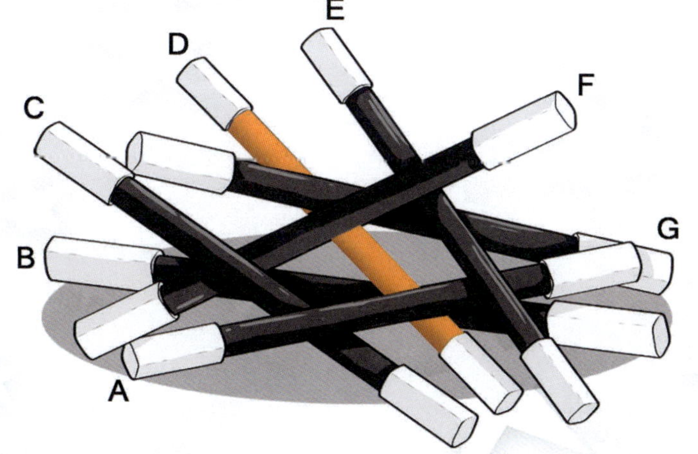

50 Through A Brick Wall

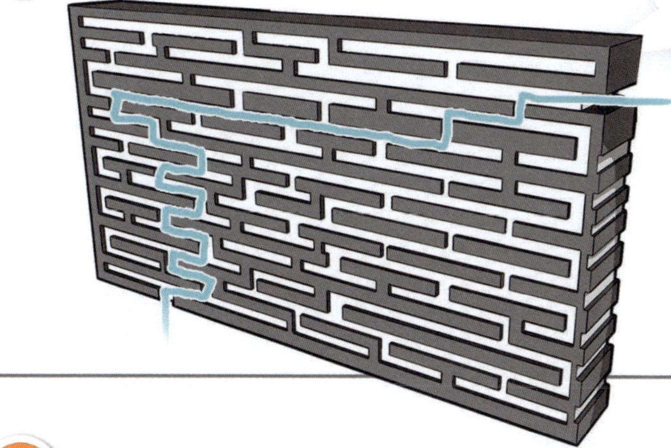

50 Knot or Knot

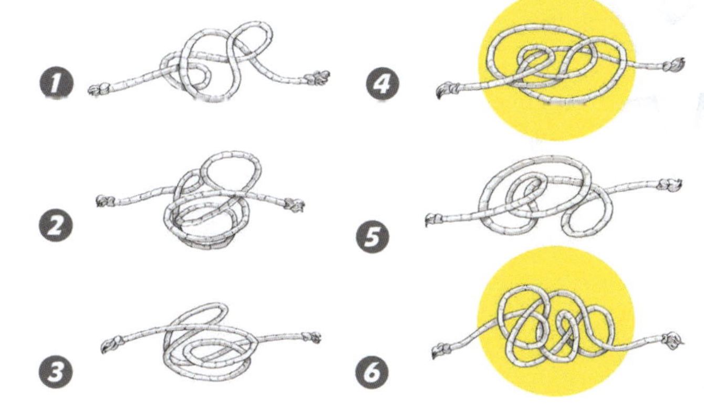

51 Where In The World

A	U	F	J	V	P	Q	A	I	S	R	D	G	X
U	I	Z	M	K	I	N	D	T	R	O	R	G	A
S	R	S	Q	Z	I	N	R	V	P	W	G	H	T
T	E	P	S	H	J	V	Z	X	E	J	X	F	O
R	L	A	C	C	C	F	Z	Q	C	E	F	B	Z
A	A	I	E	K	I	K	R	E	I	A	I	P	R
L	N	N	N	P	J	R	O	A	Q	R	M	T	P
I	D	B	G	T	B	A	L	C	N	B	O	B	D
A	I	U	L	S	R	P	N	M	I	C	G	C	Q
W	Z	S	A	I	A	V	F	P	I	L	E	A	O
T	C	K	N	T	Z	F	F	X	H	V	Y	F	Z
J	V	W	D	A	I	Q	E	D	S	F	T	O	C
K	F	P	N	L	L	M	C	A	N	A	D	A	Y
F	J	E	G	Y	P	T	D	S	Y	V	Q	Z	C

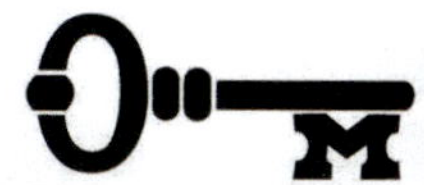

ANSWERS

52 Smoke And Mirror Maze

57 Picture Riddles

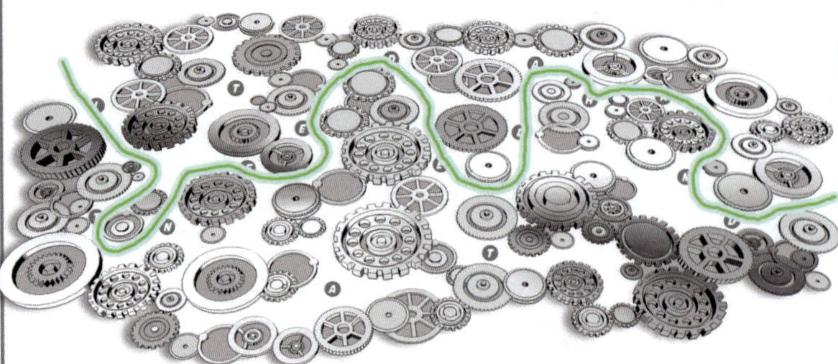

IT NEEDED A HAND!

59 Magic Art Museum

ANSWERS

61 What's Wrong

62 Snack Mix

N	U	T	S
S	T	N	U
T	S	U	N
U	N	S	T

N	A	C	H	O	S
S	H	O	A	C	N
O	N	S	C	H	A
H	C	A	S	N	O
C	S	N	O	A	H
A	O	H	N	S	C

S	O	F	T	D	R	I	N	K
I	T	N	O	K	F	S	D	R
K	R	D	S	I	N	T	O	F
F	I	S	N	T	K	O	R	D
T	D	R	I	F	O	N	K	S
N	K	O	D	R	S	F	I	T
R	N	I	K	S	T	D	F	O
O	S	K	F	N	D	R	T	I
D	F	T	R	O	I	K	S	N

65 Mystic Mirror

66 Rabbit Rescue

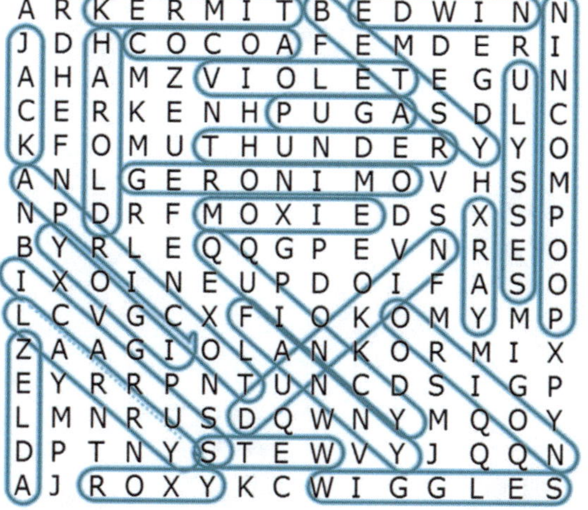

69 Note Worthy

ANSWERS

70 Traits Of A True Magician

```
T H C B M F D R G
E A O Y R C W R I
N U N Q V C V E V
T T F V H R C S I
H H I H U E D P N
U E D P M G O E G
S N E R B T N C X
I T N E L I O T L
A I T P E V B F V
S C B A P E B U Y
T K B R O K L L B
I C R E A T I V E
C J O D P U R B M
```

70 Picture Pieces

Four. It doesn't matter how many adjoining pieces there are, you only need four colors to never have two pieces of the same color touching.

73 Secret Words

1. Man overboard
2. Round of applause
3. Growing old
4. Crossroads
5. Top hat
6. Spaceship
7. Black belt in karate
8. Quarterback
9. Seventh inning stretch
10. First down
11 Hole in one
12. Halftime

75 Juggling Side Show Quiz

1. Four
2. A dog
3. Red
4. A Monkey
5. Sideshow
6. Six
7. Four
8. Blue

76 Vanishing Car

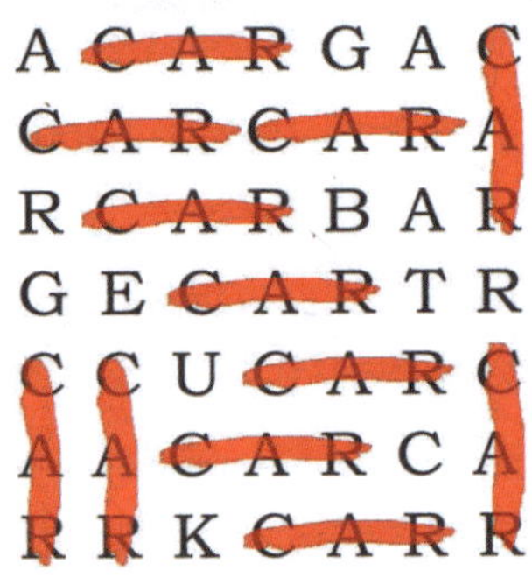

A GARBAGE TRUCK!

76 Matching Hats

77 True Magicians

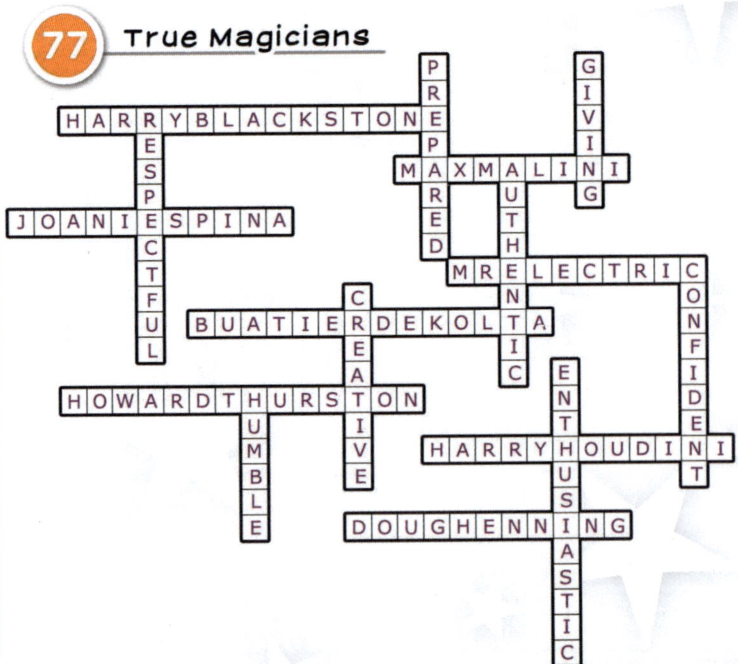